Foreign Travelers in America
1810–1935

Foreign Travelers in America
1810–1935

Advisory Editors:

Arthur M. Schlesinger, Jr.
Eugene P. Moehring

AMERICA SEEN THROUGH GERMAN EYES

ARTHUR FEILER

ARNO PRESS
A New York Times Company
New York—1974

Reprint Edition 1974 by Arno Press Inc.

Reprinted from a copy in
  The Newark Public Library

FOREIGN TRAVELERS IN AMERICA, 1810-1935
ISBN for complete set: 0-405-05440-8
See last pages of this volume for titles.

Manufactured in the United States of America

Library of Congress Cataloging in Publication Data

Feiler, Arthur, 1879-1942.
   America seen through German eyes.

   (Foreign travelers in America, 1810-1935)
   Translation of Amerika-Europa.
   Reprint of the 1928 ed. published by New Republic,
inc., New York.
   1. United States--Social condition--1918-1932.
2. United States--Economic conditions--1918-1945.
I. Title. II. Series.
HC106.3.F42 1974   309.1'73'091   73-13128
ISBN 0-405-05451-3

AMERICA
SEEN THROUGH
GERMAN EYES

DR. ARTHUR FEILER
Editor: Frankfurter Zeitung

AMERICA SEEN THROUGH GERMAN EYES

translated by
MARGARET LELAND GOLDSMITH

NEW YORK
NEW REPUBLIC, INC.
1928

To

MY WIFE

CONTENTS

PAGE

PREFACE—by *Eduard C. Lindeman* . . . xiii

INTRODUCTION : EUROPE'S MISTAKE . . . I

I: AMERICAN PROSPERITY

THE SETTLEMENT OF THE COUNTRY . . . 9

a) Urban settlement; cities in the primeval forest
—Pacific coast—Chicago—New York and the skyscrapers—Typical cities—Citizens, their city and
their home.

b) The settlement of the land : free land—Irrigation
—Farmland—The agricultural crisis—Emigration
from the rural districts—Distribution of farms,
owners and operators—The ascent on the agricultural ladder.

c) The American's environment—Rural and urban
population.

THE AUTOMOBILE 57

Its extensive use—The traffic problem—Traffic—
The automobile and the farmer—Camp life—The
will to own a car as an economic factor.

THE ACCESSIBILITY OF EDUCATION . . . 70

The wealth of educational institutions—The practical aim of education—Property has no monopoly
on education—Child labor—How students "work
their way" through college—College attendance increasing.

FIGURES OF PROSPERITY 85

Natural wealth—National wealth—National income
—Wages of labor—Purchasing power of money.

ix

II: THE AMERICAN ECONOMIC SYSTEM

PAGE

THREE ECONOMIC AREAS 93

AGRICULTURE 97
    Agricultural education—Capturing markets—National standardization—Large city banks and small provincial banks—Credit to the farmers—Elevators and warehouses—Agricultural coöperatives—Gigantic coöperatives.

TRADE, INDUSTRY AND THE PURCHASER . . 121
    Uniformity of consumption—Huge mail order houses, chain stores and "brands"—Advertisement—Service—Trusts, cartels, competition—Installment purchasing.

THE CONVEYOR SYSTEM 135
    Saving of human labor—Empty factory halls—Rationalization—The conveyor—Human labor at the machine.

THE PROCEEDS OF EFFICIENT ORGANIZATION . 145
    Ability to export despite high wages—Capital surplus and the need of capital—America provides capital to Europe.

INDUSTRIAL RELATIONS 153
    Conflicting factors—Shop Councils—I.W.W.—The "scum"—Socialism and economic democracy—The American Federation of Labor—Union shops and non-union shops—The Amalgamated Clothing Workers—The upper stratum of labor.

TRADE UNION CAPITALISM 180
    Labor banks—Employees, workers and customers as share holders.

IMMIGRATION RESTRICTIONS AND THEIR SOCIOLOGICAL CONSEQUENCES 188
    European or American development—The Immigration Law of 1924—Labor as a supporter of this law; the benefits derived by labor—The coming power of the unions.

III: THE AMERICAN WORLD

PAGE

PEOPLES, RACES AND THE NATION   .   .   .   194

    a) Americanization: The Melting Pot—Settlements
—The first steps toward Americanization.

    b) The colored people: Indians—Boycott of yellow
races—The Negro problem.

    c) German-Americans, Anglo-Americans and Amer-
icans: The Germans' struggle for existence—British
influence—The Middle Westerner.

PUBLIC LIFE   223

    Provincialism—The policy of isolation and European
pacification—Democracy   and   conservatism—The
Party System—Business politics—The country is too
prosperous—Idealistic forces.

PRIVATE LIFE AND SOCIAL FORCES   .   .   .   243

    The   Churches—Conventions—Women—Prohibition
—Emptiness.

DEVELOPMENTS OF THE FUTURE   262

    Wealth as a handicap—Wealth as a promoter of
progress—Intellectual   unrest—Youth—Budgeting—
The new form.

AND EUROPE?   276

PREFACE

Amerika-Europa created something of a sensation in Germany. The question which it proposed— What is the meaning of the New America to Old Europe?—became a topic for conversation in all circles. Here it seemed was a book which had with one sharp thrust cut through masses of exaggerated, misinformed, grotesque opinion; those who had read this book were for once discussing the problem in realistic terms. The distinguished editor of the *Frankfurter Zeitung* had presented to his people and to Europe a sharply-etched picture of life as it is actually lived in the United States; the consequences were both illuminating and cathartic. None of the many post-war European interpretations of American life had, I believed, reached an equal level of authenticity, insight, and discrimination.

Much of the above I said to the author when I discussed his book with him in Frankfurt-am-Main. It then occurred to me that a book which was capable of explaining so much about us to Germans might be useful in explaining us to ourselves. Happily, Dr. Feiler was induced to share this conviction, and still more happily, here is his book. It contains an amazing summary of facts concerning our industry, agriculture, education, prosperity, advertising, trade unions, churches, and sports. Everything is told in straightforward, almost naïve fashion—in the style of Darwin's *Voyage of the Beagle*. But Dr. Feiler does not forget that he is also the liberal editor who sees facts in relation to each other, and is under obligation to search for meanings. The interpreter's function he performs, and the prophet's, also. But even in this realm he refrains from mystifying symbolisms and continues to speak out clearly, sometimes bitingly, but always with lucidity and fair-mindedness. We have become, he thinks, "the most conservative country in the world." No great, stirring problems confront us and much of our prodigious energy is devoted to meaningless tasks. The descriptive terms which explain us most adequately are spaciousness, restlessness, loneliness, and emptiness. Of these, the most impressive to Dr. Feiler is our great "inner loneliness." His main thesis, namely that Europe will not be Americanized and that the United States is upon the verge of being transformed into a new, non-European, and in some respects unique cultural entity is, it seems to me, logically derived from the facts. Dr. Feiler does not, fortunately, attempt to placate us in the manner of some of our recent critics. He relates his observed facts, draws his conclusions, and rests his case. His great service consists in this: he has pointed out to thoughtful Americans the areas of pertinent and relevant fact. His is not a "smart" essay; indeed, it is thoroughly plain, simple even, and perhaps this is why it leads to so much fruitful reflection.

EDUARD C. LINDEMAN.

A M E R I C A
SEEN THROUGH
GERMAN EYES

INTRODUCTION

EUROPE'S MISTAKE

TO-DAY "America" is again one of Europe's most popular watchwords. "We must become like Americans" some Europeans preach—and they mean machines, gigantic factories, they mean in fact all the technical skill and unspontaneous calculations of industrial capitalism.

"Are we really to become wholly like Americans?" is asked despairingly, angrily by others—who, in turn, mean the subjection of man by machinery, the domination of materialism and of material forces; they mean the overpowering of nature and the destruction of the human soul.

A German crossing the ocean, therefore, wonders intensely whether he will really have the opportunity of gazing into the future; whether, in present-day America, he will foresee what Germany, what Europe will be like to-morrow. I am now sure that there is no greater or more dangerous mistake than this opinion.

For in reality the situation is just the reverse: Europe—I mean Central and Western Europe, for Russia which is now a special problem, and must be considered apart, is separated from the rest of Europe more completely than if it were cut off by the highest walls imaginable and outside of all European calculations—Europe will never become like America not, perhaps, because Europe does not desire this change, but because it cannot be. But whether America will some day be like Europe, whether, if Europe continues to destroy herself, America may not take possession of Europe's inheritance, is the great question of the future.

In the first place, even if we should be greatly "Americanized," Europe will never be like America. Even if an increasing number of European newspapers are abandoning their cultural traditions and their ethical sense in order to serve smart sensationalism and demagogy by adopting headlines and other methods of American journalistic technique; even if we dance to jazz music and adopt the revolting gumchewing habit, which is being increasingly abolished in the United States, just because an American concern decided that Germany was a favorable market for its products—despite all this we are still Europe, a degraded and caricatured Europe which, with confused instincts greedily accepts the worst coming from the outside world.   And do we really mean that we need America to teach us how to permeate our industrial life with all the technical subtleties and the ruthless forces of capitalism?   Machinery is our own fate, machines were created in Europe with the birth of the millions who continue to overcrowd our already overcrowded continent.   But despite our mechanical development we shall never be like America, for we lack the tangible results which nature, technical skill and the capitalistic organization have brought forth there; above all we lack the unexhausted, inexhaustible natural resources which this young country has at its disposal.   This great plenty, and the spaciousness and fullness of the country, are the fundamental factors separating Europe from America to-day.   Our destiny is meagerness and narrowness.   During the last eleven years we Germans, particularly, have let our machinery grow rusty and much sand has collected in our wheels. It is time, high time, in fact, that we cleaned them thoroughly. It is disastrous that many of those who are chiefly concerned, many of our industrialists, do not even realize that sand and rust—their sand and rust—have accumulated in our machines. But even if they finally appreciate the situation and act accordingly the fact remains that the elements producing wealth in America—aside from enormous fortunes for the few, a sufficient income for many, though not for all—could not produce more than the necessities for Europe. For this reason Europe will never be really like America. The Old World may grow to resemble the United States in its bustling activity, but it will never be like America in the results which at least partly compensate for this restlessness.

To-day America is in a transition stage. So far the country has not really found itself; it is still like a European colony, like colonial Europe. But its emancipation from Europe has begun; the World War which caused Europe to decline and increased America's wealth and power has hastened this process. To-day America is trying to find its own way, its own form.

The difference in the problems confronting America and Europe is obvious. It became particularly clear to me in a conversation with one of the most distinguished economist-statesmen in the United States. He talked enthusiastically about the country's tremendous prosperity, with the almost professional optimism which is so typically American. Large masses of American people, he emphasized, increasingly are sharing in the new products of civi-

lization, production itself is continuously increasing
—he saw hardly a shadow in this progress. "Why,
then," I asked him, "are you still making such a
strenuous effort to produce more and more? Why,
if the people are sufficiently supplied with goods of
all kinds, are you educating them to feel the need of
even more?" Obviously this question was very European. Supply and demand are coördinated; if one
increases the other must naturally follow. The suggestion that people might be satisfied with the degree
of production attained, that new technical achievements might perhaps be used not to increase consumption (for which people must labor) but to decrease hours of work, *i.e.*, to increase leisure and
freedom, probably sounded like a European's pes-
simism to this American, or perhaps like a blas-
pheming doubt of the divine cosmic system which
rules in God's own country.

After a moment's hesitation, however, he replied
and his answer was very significant. "In America,"
he told me, "the shortening of the working day is
not really the basic problem. The 8-hour day, or
even the 44-hour week, which a considerable number
of trades unions have already achieved, had to come.
But now the basic problem concerns something else:
whether the majority of men know how to use the
leisure time which is theirs above the necessary
hours required for sleep. And as yet"—the man
facing me had become noticeably thoughtful—"we
have experienced no real success in the solution of
this problem."

So the tasks confronting Europe and America at
least to-day are widely differentiated. It is our task
to regulate our meagerness, as it were, so that no
matter how extensive a mechanization of life this

meagerness may imply for our people there may nevertheless be justice and human dignity.

America, on the other hand, is confronted with a much happier problem; to give to her plenty and not to poverty a content and a form. "Man does not become valuable merely by living in a warm house and having sufficient food. But his house must be well heated and he must be well fed if the higher nature is to assert itself." The second part of this quotation from Schiller is indicative of Europe; the first part (before the "but") might have been said of America—as of any colonial country which has completed its primary colonization and must now consider what it will do with itself next.

It is quite possible for a colony to surpass the mother continent for good or for evil. But a colony may also become like the mother country. In time a colony may even resemble the mother country in its problems and exigencies. For despite the extent to which deluded Europe ruined herself during the War and the post-war period, despite the extent to which the gulf separating European meagerness and American plenty has been widened—it must be borne in mind that America's plenty and spaciousness are not assured for all times and that, one day, America in this respect may possibly become like Europe.

I. AMERICAN PROSPERITY

AMERICAN CITIES

WASTE is the outstanding motto of the American economic system, just as it is typical of all colonial economic systems. Natural resources are more than plentiful, but human beings, who could turn them into useful products, are scarce. Raw materials are cheap, but the labor necessary to produce and finish them is all the more expensive. Over and over again, therefore, one observes a waste of raw materials, a waste which is incomprehensible to a European and especially to a German, whom the rationing system of the War and the poverty of the post-war years have taught economy to the point of stinginess. In restaurants and sometimes in private homes food in such quantities is thrown recklessly away that the waste from these overflowing tables might well nourish a good many people in impoverished Europe. Torn suits or underclothing, which we should mend and wear again as a matter of course, are discarded in America, because it is cheaper to buy new clothes than to have old ones repaired. On the outskirts of the cities there are dumps of derelict machinery, where old wagons are rusting away because it is too expensive to have them carted off. For the same reason old newspapers or rags and dilapidated household utensils, which have been thrown away in the Ghetto of New York, are simply raked together and burned, because fire is the cheapest method of getting rid of these things. In large California fruit-packing establishments the ripest and most delicious fruits are cast aside, as they would not remain fresh

9

if they were transported to the East, and no one living near the plant would consider it worth his while to come and get them.

America has been more wasteful of her forests than of anything else. Like the advancing pioneers, who in colonial days exterminated whole herds of buffaloes so that to-day specimens of these animals can be seen only in National Parks and in Zoölogical Gardens, like these pioneers who cleared the forests so thoroughly of their animals that now venison or wild poultry is not eaten at all by American city dwellers, in the same way the trail, which the settlement of the American Continent has blazed, is indicated by the destruction of forest lands. The original settler cut down as much wood as he needed to build his log cabin. Then, to clear a plot of ground which he could cultivate, he set fire to the trees around his new home. All this is in the past, but even now America is far from administering her forests efficiently. The Government is actively engaged in an attempt to plant them afresh, a plan which was zealously sponsored by Carl Schurz. Traveling through Colorado and California one frequently sees barren hills on which young trees have been planted: these future forests seem to emphasize how much has actually been destroyed. The consumption of lumber in America is enormous. In districts where coal or petroleum or natural gas are not easily available, wood is widely used as fuel. Residence houses all over America are usually made of wood and in smaller cities this is always the case. The paper consumption of newspapers, which on Sundays especially seem like enormous bundles, is prodigious. And all exhortations to be more saving are of no avail when economy does not pay. If in

a city, with a million population or more, a block of
houses is torn down to make room for a skyscraper
the lumber falling from the old houses, as well as
the huge wooden scaffolding used to erect the new
building, is simply burned up: it is not possible to
make use of this old wood. For a long time the
United States has been forced to fall back upon
Canada's enormous forest reserves. There are even
some newspapers in the western part of America
which use Swedish paper. In the meantime forest
fires are still doing their deadly work, when sparks
from a rushing train are blown into the forests or
when picnickers forget to extinguish their camp fires.
Again and again one sees mere skeletons of trees with
charred branches pointing to the sky. Forest lands
which are privately owned and are not controlled by
the State or National Governments are being ruthlessly chopped down all the time, mile after mile.
Little thought is given to reforestation. This is left
largely to Nature, who bountifully provides for the
next generation of trees. For the forest-wealth of
this country is still enormous. In the Eastern States
as well as in the South the cutting down of forests
has been going on for decades, but in the West, and
particularly in the Northwest, there are vast forest
lands which are still practically untouched. In 1920
the timber produced in the State of Washington
was valued at 191 million dollars, the total amount
produced in America being valued at 1,299 millions.
The previous record was made in Louisiana, where
timber worth 137 millions was produced in one year.
Oregon, with a production valued at 121 million dollars, almost reached Louisiana's level. Despite these
high figures the systematic production of lumber in
these Western States is only just beginning. The

Northwest has only been attracting settlers from other parts of the country for the last twenty years. Washington and Oregon are still two of the most sparsely populated States of the Union. A few hours away from the great port cities of the North-west there are still densely wooded primeval forests which no human foot has ever trod. While I was in Portland I rode out to see a lumber camp on the edge of this great virgin forest. The things I saw there were more helpful than almost anything else towards an understanding of the growth and evolution of a colonial country.

In Portland we had been told that by bus we would reach Longview in two hours and a half; that we would find a hotel in which we could spend the night quite comfortably, and that the next morning a lumber train would take us into the virgin forest. What would a German naturally look forward to after such a description? He would expect narrow primitive roads and then a small primitive village, like so many in the Black Forest. There he would expect to find a small village inn and a land-lord who might be persuaded to give one primitive accommodation for the night. Instead of all this the bus glides along a broad and well-oiled asphalt road—it is the highway to Seattle. It is true that the ride was lonely enough. We drove past silent farms, small saw-mills and modest little towns. We passed orchards and cornfields and grazing cattle, but otherwise the road winds through silent forests, which are inaccessible because of their thick under-growth. At the end of the trip a great surprise awaited us. We did not find the few little sleepy houses we had expected to see at the edge of the virgin forest. Longview is a city, with a hotel the like of which does not exist in Germany: two hundred rooms with as many bathrooms and every other modern convenience. Two dozen cars are parked outside the hotel. There is a business street with plentiful shop windows, a street vivid with glaring electric lights. There is an office district, an industrial district, a hospital, a few schoolhouses, a Y. M. C. A. Community Center with a gymnasium, a swimming pool, a library, a reading room, etc. There is also a "four-story $250,000 theater building," as a circular briefly and conscientiously informs us. In German this means a moving picture theater, four stories high, which cost a million marks to build (for from coast to coast one can never admire, or not admire, any public building in this country without being told at once how much it cost). In Longview there are broad lawns and wide avenues and an even larger park in the making. Built around this park and separated from the business district by green lawns is the residential section of the town, consisting exclusively of single houses for each separate family. Some of these residence districts include modest workers' homes; others, judging from the somewhat larger houses, are inhabited by people who are better off; while still other districts consist of very comfortable homes. But in all of these residence districts the single house prevails. There are only two or three apartment houses for the bachelors of Longview. Everywhere the plumbing system and the electric lighting plant are in excellent condition. All the houses have their own telephones, garages and cars. And this was the Black Forest village which we expected to find. Early the next morning a newspaper reporter came to interview me—one cannot avoid this fate, which is shared by all foreigners visiting America, even on the edge of the virgin forest!

Less than three years ago there was nothing here but pasture land and a few lonely farms. Longview's first street was laid out in August, 1922. In February, 1923, the first building site was sold and in February, 1924, the settlement was incorporated as a town. By April, 1925, Longview could boast of 278 shops and two banks with total deposits amounting to more than a million dollars credited to more than four thousand depositors. At this time there were thirteen hundred children of school age and thirty-one teachers in Longview, 1,446 residence houses had been built, or were in the process of being finished, and Longview had a population of seven thousand souls. It is planned, like a decree from heaven, that Longview shall have 25,000 inhabitants five years after the date of founding the town, and five years after that the residents are to number 50,000. What has happened here? A large lumber company, in business in the south, realized that in that part of the country the end of its activities was in sight. The company had exhausted all the forest lands it owned in there, and no timber was left to be cut down. The question was, should the company be dissolved? This seemed wrong, for the employees, as well as the accumulated capital, had to be put to some use. The company, therefore, followed the example of others and moved bag and baggage to the Northwest, where extensive forest lands had not yet been opened up. Here the company was able to buy vast tracts of land for a song, as the country round about was practically uninhabited and it was necessary only to buy up a few worthless farms. Then the company began to exploit the new territory on a large scale. With its own railroad the company broke into the virgin forest: in train-loads of twenty-four cars or more the proud trees, often over a meter in diameter, were transported from the forest above, where they had been hewn, into the valley below. In this valley, about fifty kilometers from the forest, on the banks of the river, the company erected a saw-mill of huge dimensions. The town of Longview really came into being because of this mill.

One might almost say that Longview now has a sister town. In the forest itself the lumbermen live in simple shacks, four men in a shack. These are built four in a row and six rows deep. In the center of each block of shacks there is one, larger than the others, which is used as a kitchen and messroom. Here, incidentally, excellent meals are served, for good food is the only advantage which will hold these restless fellows, whose wages are as high as $3.60 to $6.00, and for particularly difficult work even $10.00 a day, but who, nevertheless, do not put up with this life for long. The lumbermen's shacks are built on train wheels, and when the work has been finished in one clearing the railroad tracks are laid a few miles further into the forest, the engine is hitched onto the shacks and they are moved to another place where work is to begin anew. It became necessary to furnish the married lumbermen with more stable homesteads, and their shacks were left standing in a large clearing of the forest. Then some primitive streets, consisting of a few rows of houses, were built, and in less than a year Ryderwood came into being, a cross between a lumber

camp and a town. Now there are four hundred
houses for a little less than two thousand people;
there is a large community store where one can buy
everything from canned food to silk stockings or
wardrobe trunks; there is a community center and a
schoolhouse. A moving picture theater and a hotel
are being built. So far Ryderwood still belongs to
the company. Some day perhaps, when most of the
lumber has been cut away and the distance to the
forest has become too great, Ryderwood may be
abandoned. Then the houses will be evacuated and
carted away to be burned or thrown away—it really
does not matter what happens to them then.

In Colorado, on a long journey up the Rocky
Mountains, I saw the history of this country reflected in the crumbling settlements of its pioneers:
the gold-diggers. They were the earliest white men
to enter this wilderness. At first they looked for the
tempting metal in the river bed. Afterwards an increasing number of small mines were opened up, so
that gold, silver, lead and other metals could be secured more quickly. Again and again, and in dozens
of places, the ground was broken so that the veins
of ore became accessible. For a time these young
mines seem to have prospered; small and large towns
sprang up around their pits. But when the upper
veins had been exhausted, possible profits did not
seem to warrant the cost of digging deeper, and the
mines were abandoned. The mining machinery, the
houses around the pits, were simply left behind, and
now they are gradually decaying. The wooden
buildings are slowly falling to pieces; here and there
a tramp may be seen, living rent free in one of these
tumble-down shacks and raising chickens in the old

boiler house of the mine. The settlements in the river valley met the same fate. The towns which survived have become summer resorts for the inhabitants of the neighboring cities. The income of these resorts depends entirely upon their summer visitors. Perhaps Ryderwood, now a lumbermen's settlement in the virgin forest, may one day have the same destiny. Perhaps, on the other hand, Ryderwood may be the beginning of a new metropolis. Everything is possible.

Longview at any rate is to-day a city with a life of its own. To attract its employees and to keep them in Longview the company had the town laid out on a grand scale by specialized town planners. Now the town continues to develop along these lines spontaneously. There are many young people in Longview. It is possible that the saw-mill will expand to include finishing industries, and the establishment of other industrial concerns may follow. An experimental flax field shows that Longview is trying to progress—a new city is growing up on the edge of the virgin forest.

Another picture: Los Angeles, the center of southern California, a city which is in keen competition with San Francisco for the leadership of the state, was only an unpretentious medium-sized town in a lonely country twenty-five years ago. Now Los Angeles has a population of a million, and so far the city is by no means contemplating any limit to its expansion and growth. "Why Los Angeles will become the World's Greatest City" is the title of one of the many "boosting" pamphlets published in various forms and styles for the benefit of people with all kinds of interests. This slogan reflects the atmosphere of speculative enthusiasm which one can sense everywhere in this part of the world.

In 1900 Los Angeles' population was ten times as large as it was in 1880. This is not so very surprising, as the city was extremely small at first. But since 1900 it has again grown ten times larger, and now the population statistics of the city show the following picture:

Year	City	County
1850	1,610	3,530
1860	4,385	11,333
1870	5,728	15,309
1880	11,183	33,381
1890	50,395	101,454
1900	102,479	170,298
1910	319,198	504,131
1920	576,673	936,455
1924 [1]	1,073,995	1,746,300

Other statistics reflect this growth of the city in the same way. In 1900 bank clearings in Los Angeles amounted to 123 million dollars, by 1910 they had risen to 811 million, by 1920 to 3,994 million and in 1924 they amounted to 7,194 million dollars. Bank deposits rose from 383 million dollars early in 1920 to 983 million early in 1925.[2] Statistics showing the number of building permits issued are more illuminating in this connection than any others:

[1] The figures up to and including 1920 are official Census figures. The figure for 1924 is an estimate made by the Chamber of Commerce, which may be somewhat enthusiastic, but at any rate this figure is about the average of the various estimates at hand.

[2] Bank deposits for the whole State totaled 970 million in the middle of 1915; 2,044 million in the middle of 1920; 2,969 million in the middle of 1924. These figures indicate an increase by two billion dollars during the last 10 years.

Year	Number	Value
1919	13,344	$28,253,619
1920	25,555	$60,023,600
1921	37,206	$82,761,386
1922	47,387	$121,206,787
1923	62,548	$200,133,181
1924	51,134	$150,147,516
Total in 6 years	237,174	$642,526,089

These figures show that during the six years since the war Los Angeles, which is by no means one of America's largest cities, has considered itself in a position to spend two and three-quarters billion marks on building operations. This is not an unparalleled instance. The number of building permits issued by an industrial city like Detroit is almost as high (six hundred million dollars were spent during the same six years, though in Detroit more permits were issued for office buildings than for residences). All over America, from New York to the Pacific, building operations are enormous. There seems to be a feverish desire to rebuild and to enlarge. But concerning the point which I particularly want to emphasize here, the growth and evolution of a colonial country, Los Angeles seems to me to be typical. Los Angeles is the trading center of an agricultural district which is developing prosperously and quickly. The city is not situated directly on the sea, but San Pedro, 25 kilometers away, a town which could not have developed by itself, has been taken into partnership, as it were. The municipality of Los Angeles rebuilt this little harbor into a great seaport, and a special railroad was laid to connect Los Angeles with San Pedro. Thus Los Angeles created a direct communication with the Pacific. The surrounding agricultural district and this direct connection with the sea are the two most important factors which have contributed to the growth of the city. So far Los Angeles has very little industry of its own and this lack is a weakness. Only the moving picture industry, at Hollywood, has developed on a large scale (the Chamber of Commerce estimates the annual output of this industry at 168 million dollars). Two other factors, however, really shaped this city's character: the climate, and the oil wells, which are located in a large area extending to the coast and farther north. Oil is being produced even at the bottom of the sea. Around Los Angeles innumerable derricks are crowded together. Some of the hills around the city are so closely covered with them that they seem to rise into the sky like some strange forest, while real trees are dying all about them. These oil wells insure an increasing population, for they attract settlers to Los Angeles. Oil is also a constant stimulus to trade. But these are not the only benefits Los Angeles derives from her oil. The very fact that oil exists furnishes the city with speculative profits and speculative hopes: the story of individuals who became millionaires over night is a constant temptation to others. Besides, the city has a climate which always attracts Easterners, just as Italy attracts the Germans. Almost every day in the year the sun shines brilliantly. There is no winter, and yet the evenings are always refreshingly cool. Under this ever-radiant sky the profusion of flowers is gorgeous beyond any description. These attractions have drawn swarms of people to California and especially to Los Angeles. All colonial settlements, like California, possess unearned wealth, for the settlers are mature and fitted for life when they arrive in their new home—the mother country, in other words, loses the capital invested in their upbringing, whereas the colonial country receives this capital as a gift. California and Los Angeles were especially blessed. Not all their settlers began to earn their living when they reached the Coast; many of them, who were wealthy when they came, brought their capital with them from the East or the Middle West and spent it in developing the Coast.

The process of building, therefore, usually a means to an end, is here an end in itself, and a continuous source of increasing wealth. An American economist expressed the old economic problem of a modern city in the cleverly exaggerated formula: "As a matter of fact we really earn our living in a city by taking in each other's washing." Similarly one could claim that in a city like Los Angeles people live by building houses for each other. Directly or indirectly every one participates in these building operations, not only the wage-earners doing the actual work, but the banks which finance these enterprises, the shipping companies which transport the raw materials, the furniture manufacturers who deliver the necessary furniture. It is not the actual building, but rather the sales and speculations in real estate which yield the greatest returns. A man discovered oil near the city and became wealthy. His successor on the land burned up the oil, sold the site as a building lot, and became even more wealthy. The business districts are constantly expanding, and are beginning to include some of the former residential quarters of the city. Dwelling houses in these quarters are placed on wheels and are carted away to a more quiet district where real estate is cheaper. It is the real estate men who are molding

Los Angeles, just as they once shaped the development of cities in Germany. But in Germany, since the great expansion of our cities in the seventies, real estate men have been crowding masses of the population into prison-like, undignified tenement houses, built along treeless, airless streets, in which the sun seldom shines—streets which for miles follow one after the other, disfiguring our cities. Never did I realize so poignantly of how much joy and freedom this wrong city planning has robbed our people during the last half century until I came to America. It is true that in the center of Los Angeles, with its Japanese, Chinese, Mexican, and colored districts, groups of people live closely huddled together. But these people are only a small part of the whole population. The others live in the light. According to the census of 1920 every 4.6th individual lived in a separate house, while the average family included 3.6 members. About 76 per cent of the new residential houses registered in 1923 were inhabited by single families; 19 per cent of the homes registered were duplex houses and only 5 per cent were apartment houses. In California, where the one-story houses predominate, these duplex houses are usually built next to each other. Often four or six of them are built together and form a so-called bungalow court. In other sections of the country they are built one above the other; that is to say there is a separate front door and a separate staircase for the families living on either floor of the house. This type of duplex is familiar to us, for it is like some of the houses in Westphalia. Even the fact that 19 per cent of the houses are duplex is surprising, for in Los Angeles the single house is the predominating type of residence. Even wage-earners, who earn relatively high wages, live in single houses. The popularity of separate residences has caused a tremendous expansion of the city. For this reason building and contracting companies have gone into business all around the city. They make plans for the opening up of new districts, they build asphalt roads and plant palms along the sidewalks. They lay pipes for the plumbing system, they install the gas, electric light and telephone. Not until these preliminaries are finished do they begin selling the separate lots. Sometimes these companies build houses at their own cost, which are sold when they are absolutely complete. "For Sale," "For Rent"— hundreds, yes, thousands of times one can see these signs in front of shops or houses, or posted up in the lots themselves. Speculation is the great thing. Every one does it. Some day the boom may slacken but so far optimism has won.

This atmosphere of speculation extends to the beach, where the same speculators have built resorts with the same speculative methods. "Venice" is the name given to one of these resorts, where an attempt was made to create an artificial lagoon city in miniature, to imitate the canals and the Rialto. But despite these efforts Antonio and Shylock did not come. Probably in the end this enterprise proved to be too expensive. Other ventures have been all the more successful. For miles and miles similar resorts have been created by speculators. When you have finally managed to escape from their amusement parks, the confusion and noise of their narrow streets, and you think that, at last, you have found solitude, that you have gotten away from the atmosphere of speculation, you will suddenly find the beginnings of new streets staked out in the sand-dunes. And at the end of a path, where nothing is visible but sand and grass and sky, a huge sign will fling these proud words at you: "This is the center of a new town."

The settlement of the West is still so young that one can study the changes which are occurring as clearly as though they were described in a textbook. Farther East, on the other hand, in older sections of the United States, these changes have already been absorbed and are now vital components of the country as a whole. And yet in all American cities the same change, the same evolution, is occurring. A few "automobile hours" from Chicago there are cities which, like Longview, are entirely artificial creations of industry. Take Gary, the steel city, as an example, which was founded in 1909 and which by 1924 had a population of 65,000. Gary's business district includes buildings of various sizes, but the residence section, where single houses are imbedded in green trees and gardens, is peaceful and quiet. In general the town looks like any of the older cities in America. On the outskirts of Gary, however, much space for building is still available, and asphalt streets leading nowhere in all directions tempt people to put up their house there. As another example there is an oil city which, judging by the newness of its houses, is even younger than Gary. The entire town, including the residence section and the huge oil plant, was built on worthless swamp and underbrush country. And now this worthless land is cut through by streams, which have already been completed, and soon houses will be built along them.

Above all there is Chicago itself with the following population:

1870 298,977
1890 1,099,850
1910 2,185,283
1924 2,942,605

(The suburbs, not included in the above, had a population of 499,596 in 1920.)

These figures indicate that Chicago has long since passed its "Los Angeles period" of development, but the city is still growing at a fantastic rate. The forms which this expansion is taking are also fantastic. The avenue along Lake Michigan had become too narrow to accommodate the immense traffic, so the lake is being filled up for about a half mile along its edge, though without perceptibly encroaching upon the lake itself which is almost as big as Bavaria. This artificial landslide will give Chicago a magnificent boulevard, with beautiful walks, large golf links, an inland harbor for sailboats, etc. Other streets, too, will have to be widened, and so whole blocks of houses are being torn down. Others are being cut right through the middle and are left standing half their original size. Sometimes, if there is room, houses are simply moved back a few feet, for in Chicago as in other parts of the United States, house moving is a regular business carried out by specialists. It is relatively simple to move plain wooden houses. If they are too large they are sawn apart into two or three sections which are moved separately and are put together again when they have been transported to their destination. I saw an eight-story office building which had been moved in this way. It took several weeks, but during this time the plumbing, gas and electric lighting system continued to function normally. Even during the move itself business went on as usual. Hesitation or unsurmountable technical difficulties are not recognized as realities in this city, which is constantly changing, as it continues to attract more and more inhabitants. In 1920 the population of Chicago included 800,000 foreign born whites and 100,000 Negroes. These two groups constituting a third of Chicago's total population, seem to move to and fro in the city in never ending confusion. At first they live detached from the rest of the population in a section which they have built up by themselves. When one group of foreigners leaves this district for a better one, another takes its place: Germans, Jews from eastern Europe, Poles, Italians, Mexicans, and finally the Negroes, who, when they move into a district, cause all the whites to move away. In a very short time the streets become quite "black." There are really evil districts in Chicago, especially near the stockyards, whence noxious vapors poison the air for miles about. So far there is no right which can stand up against the sanctity of property belonging to the great meat-packing concerns. They own the little stream which flows through the stockyards district and they do not hesitate to use it as a drain. The packers do not care whether the foul air from this stream chokes the poor people living in the neighborhood.

Yet in other ways the municipal government is trying to improve conditions. Enormous parks have been laid out in various sections of the city, parks with zoölogical gardens, with wonderful hothouses, with playgrounds and bandstands for public concerts. All these benefits the population can have for nothing. On the outskirts the city has purchased large forests which are protected as "forest reserves." Here there are wooden tables, places to make camp fires, and running water. Picnickers go out to these woods by the thousands to have a good time. Within the city limits people can have free swims in the lake. Above all, even in the most densely populated quarters the streets are wide, the houses low. Tenement houses are very rare. Even in crowded Chicago there were 335,777 houses for 623,912 families in 1920. In other words, on an average, there were only eight individuals to every house. Only downtown, in the financial, office, and department-store district, do skyscrapers rise above the streets, ten, twenty or thirty stories high.

Skyscrapers are the first thing which a foreigner sees when he comes to America. The dizzy loftiness of the Manhattan skyline seems to loom above the arriving ship like a citadel raised on high by the cyclops. At first no details can be distinguished. The picture is seen as a whole, an amazing agglomeration of iron and cement. A spire, a tower, or a dome, are conspicuous here or there, and one building is seen to be twice as high as its neighbor. The whole fantastic picture seems to have been jumbled together promiscuously with no fixed plan, and this very irregularity of the scene makes it all the more impressive. Wilhelm Schafer has called early German romanesque cathedrals "Castles of the Saviour" and, with a libelous cynicism, American skyscrapers have been called "Cathedrals of Commerce." It is indeed appropriate that often their lack of a definite style is hidden behind gothic scrolls which are pasted onto their walls. Occasionally, on Broadway, one may see a pathetic little church, which has remained standing. By comparison its steeple no longer points to heaven.   In Chicago a church has even been built on top of a skyscraper: on the ground floor of this same building neckties and straw hats can be bought, higher up there are twelve stories filled with offices of various kinds, and on the fourteenth floor, there is the church.   Capitalism turned into stone—these buildings are the embodiment of capital's unrestrained power.

As a matter of fact in New York skyscrapers were a necessity.   On the narrow island at the mouth of the Hudson, it was necessary to make room for a grandiose concentration of financial and commercial enterprises.   It was impossible to spread out.   The narrow island could not be enlarged, so that expansion had to proceed skywards.   Partly because of their egregious vanity other American cities imitated this method of expansion, even if their geographical position did not compel them to do so.   Why shouldn't Y-town have skyscrapers if X-town has them?   Later a positive reason for skyscrapers developed.   These superstructures made it possible to crowd business districts into a relatively narrow space.   To facilitate business everything is built close together.   It is only a step from the bank to the stock exchange, from the office of a wholesale trading house to the bank, from the headquarters of a large factory to the lawyer's office, or to the luncheon club.   The express elevator carries one swiftly up to one's destination.   Short distances are convenient, they save time and are efficient.   This efficiency created a new manner of living.   It separated the places where an American works and where he lives, divided his day into hours of work and leisure.   In the same way this efficiency gradually created a new style of architecture, which is becoming more and more general. The skyscrapers of the large American cities are a result of efficiency. It is true that fictitious gothic towers and poorly proportioned "flatiron" buildings are still being erected. It will probably take American cities a long time to overcome the ugliness of their "Main Streets," where houses of all sizes, of every conceivable style or lack of style, stand next to each other. But now, singly, or in blocks, new buildings of a magnificent grandeur are being erected. These new buildings are gigantic in their dimensions, but well proportioned: they are real houses with real foundations and a real roof. Their architecture is genuine and sincere and shows a magnificent coördination of purpose, style and material. This new architecture which is building skyscrapers for bank palaces, stations, grain elevators, and other enterprises necessary to a modern city, is a real art and a great cultural contribution from America. Some day, without a doubt, it will find its expression in Europe. Any one who has seen Park Avenue in New York, and this is only one of many examples, will shudder when he thinks of the Kurfuersten-Damm in Berlin. Beauty can emerge even when millions of people are being crowded into a small space.

But New York, with its enormous population (in 1920 it was larger than London), is not America. New York is only the narrow gateway leading to the great American Continent. A quarter of New York's population (1,991,547) was born in Europe. If the suburbs are excluded, the proportion is even higher. These immigrants landed in America and stuck to the port of entry. There are 480,000 Russians, chiefly Russian Jews. Their ghetto in New York looks just like the Jewish quarter in Vilna or

in Whitechapel.   There are 390,000 Italians and
their washing, dangling between the houses, waves
in the breezes just as it does in Naples.   There are
200,000 Irish, 200,000 Germans, 150,000 Poles and
125,000 Austrians.   These foreigners, as well as
swarms of others of all nationalities, all colors, all
races and faiths, live in New York, closely crowded
together and separated from the rest of the population.   They are exposed to exploitation in every
form; they are still faced with the problem of fighting their way into the real America.   Often it is only
their children who succeed in winning this fight.

The real America lies farther inland, in the cities
having a million population, more or less, and in the
smaller towns.   Evil slums can be seen in cities, to
which some industrial enterprise has brought foreign
workers by carloads so as to exploit them systematically.   In these slums, like the ones in Cleveland, the
little houses swarm with all kinds of foreigners.
New shacks are crowded even into the narrow spaces
which originally separated these houses.   Sheds are
turned into dwellings, sometimes a second or even a
third story is built on top of them.   The result is a
maze of narrow alleys crowded in the evening with
children and with untidy women, wearing the wide
jackets and the large shawls typical of their homes
somewhere in eastern Europe.   It is indeed a dreary
picture of exploited poverty.   In places, however,
where this first stage of misery has been overcome,
the situation is entirely different.   Take for instance
a city like Milwaukee, "German" Milwaukee in the
"German" State of Wisconsin.   The river valley is
a tremendous industrial district.   For a long distance
there is one plant after another, but on the hills
rising from this valley and extending to the beauti-

ful shores of the lake, is a residential district with broad streets. The people who live here do not remember the cramped meagerness of Europe. The houses, except in the congested center of the town, usually have five rooms, kitchen and bath, electric light, gas for cooking and a garage on the premises. Similarly favorable conditions also prevail in the older, less prosperous districts, which are inhabited largely by wage-earners, except that here duplex houses are more general. The Poles live in such a district and I wonder whether Mr. Klabustensky, who is perhaps employed in a large tannery, ever dreamed of such luxuries when he lived in old Europe? Adjoining this part of town are Milwaukee's newer districts where the wealthy upper stratum, the middle class and more prosperous workers live. This part of Milwaukee is like a real garden city, with trim single houses. The people in them are living in light and freedom.

This is America, for this is an approximate picture of all American cities. They differ only in the details conditioned by a city's geographical situation. Fundamentally all American cities are alike from coast to coast, whether they have a population of half a million, a hundred thousand or ten thousand. They are alike in their original plan, in the architecture of their houses. Only California, with its bungalows, is reminiscent of the Spanish period. These are one-storied, straight-walled houses with few windows and a flat roof. But among them one frequently sees a colonial house with the porch on the level with the ground and the slender pillars supporting the gabled roof. This colonial house is always the same, whether it stands in a New York suburb or in a town on the Pacific Coast. Whenever a novel style of house begins to become popular the new architectural tendency may be seen in houses from coast to coast.

All this is due to the fact that American cities have no past. They have only a present and a future, and are really settlements in a new colonial country: colonial cities for colonials. And it is a fact that these people remain colonials even if their ancestors have been American citizens for generations. Their attitude towards their city, towards the house in which they live, is a colonial attitude and not a European one.

"We don't build houses, but commodities with which we can speculate," a clever scholar complained to me in Chicago. It seemed like an illustration of this bitter phrase, when the same evening a wealthy business man, who owns one of the most beautiful homes in the city, explained to me with quiet objectivity, how much the value of real estate in his part of town had risen in the course of a few years. He told me that soon he would probably be obliged to move, but that when the time came he would not only have lived rent-free, but that he would make a considerable profit on his house as well. Even if a man in a colonial country owns the house in which he lives, he does not feel settled. It is impossible to live in a district where offices instead of residence houses and gardens are being built. This change in districts is taken into account, and the more one can hasten the process the more one is able to speed up the rise in value of one's own real estate. A few private citizens in a small city had given a site of land for the building of a university. A tablet records this gift to coming generations. "They were good business men," the professor, who was acting as my guide told me, "for the land which they retained was not really valuable until this institution had been built." This is why cities advertise themselves so widely and why private individuals provide the money for this advertising. Usually the Chamber of Commerce is the organization which performs these functions for the city. In smaller towns especially the Chamber includes not only business men but physicians, lawyers, professors, etc., as well. This group of private citizens works out the plans for furthering the city's business and launches the campaigns. In one year the San Francisco Chamber of Commerce spent $400,000 to "sell" the city (which is so magnificent that it wouldn't seem to need this advertising). The real purpose of this campaign was to compete with a similar one launched by Los Angeles. In Portland people complained to me that they could not possibly keep up with the money San Francisco was spending on advertising. Local patriotism and private speculation are on the same level and are always gloriously in harmony. This system of speculation has derived a tremendous impetus from the fact that so far an increase in speculative activities has always been successful. In New York I saw a gigantic new bank palace—I cannot quite remember whether it was fifteen or twenty-five stories high. Every possible convenience for the employees had been provided for in this building. As is usual there were large dining and club rooms, a reading room and a dispensary. Besides there was a large hall, fitted out with a stage, to enable the employees to give moving picture shows, concerts, dramatic performances or dances. On the roof there was a tennis court and room for other sports. The elevator in this building did not stop at the second and third floors, which were still unoccupied—this valuable space was being reserved for the future expansion of the bank's business. This, too, is symbolic of the development of American cities.

But it is not only speculation, it is something deeper which makes the American city dweller so unsettled, despite the fact that he often owns the house in which he lives. In "Main Street," Sinclair Lewis's popular novel, there is a passage which points out this unsettled attitude: "The citizen of the prairie drifts always westward. It may be because he is the heir of ancient migrations—and it may be because he finds within his own spirit so little adventure that he is driven to seek it by changing his horizon. The towns remain unvaried, yet the individual faces alter like classes in colleges. The Gopher Prairie jeweler sells out, for no discernible reason, and moves on to Alberta or the State of Washington, to open a shop precisely like his former one, in a town precisely like the one he has left. There is, except among professional men and the wealthy, small permanence either of residence or occupation. A man becomes farmer, grocer, town policeman, garageman, restaurant-owner, postmaster, insurance-agent, and farmer all over again, and the community more or less patiently suffers from his lack of knowledge in each of his experiments."

Later I shall again mention this American restlessness, this lack of repose. It expresses some inner void, and is most symptomatic of the modern American's frame of mind. I only allude to this dissatisfaction here to prevent misunderstanding, for a European might think that so many separate homes would imply that Americans feel settled, and this is

not the case.   These wooden houses are not the
homes of successive generations, they are not filled
with traditions and memories.   The essential thing is
that a home shall be comfortable, that the kitchen,
furnace and bathroom shall be fitted out with every
modern convenience.   When people can afford it
they cheerfully exchange their house for one which
is larger, more up to date or more convenient.
Migration from one part of a city, or from one city
to another, goes on all the time.

Domestic help is so scarce and so expensive that
apartment houses, huge buildings with a number
of small apartments, are becoming more numerous.
According to the magnitude of the rent these apartments are equipped with all kinds of conveniences,
so that domestic labor can be reduced to a minimum.
In some of these houses the apartments are furnished, in some of them dinner is served from a
common kitchen.   This type of residence is the
transition to the apartment hotel.   Apartments are
chiefly popular among unattached people, or older
couples whose children have already left home.
Families with children want a house of their own.
This desire to give the children a home is one of the
most vital incentives causing Americans to work so
hard.   Sometimes people complain that the American
wage-earner spends his entire income, and accumu-
lates no savings for his old age.   But for his house,
at least, he is forced to save money, for he must
regularly pay his installments, as well as the interest
on the capital, every month.

The American wants a house for his children.
This desire gives his hard work a significance and a
content.   In general he has been able to fulfill this
desire to an extent which we Germans can hardly

grasp. Official statistics, compiled for 1920, showed that 24,351,676 families in America lived in 20,-697,204 dwellings. This means that, on an average, eighty-five out of every one hundred families in the United States lived in a separate house. If New York were excluded, where on an average 15.5 individuals live in one house (in Manhattan this average is as high as 30.2) the picture would be even more favorable. Other official statistics show the ownership conditions of these houses: 12.95 per cent were rented, but 10.58 per cent were owned by the families living in them. These figures indicate furthermore that only 4.06 per cent were mortgaged and that 6.52 per cent were free from debt. These facts are of the utmost importance for American life as a whole—they are one of the great symbols of American prosperity.

THE SETTLEMENT OF THE LAND

To an American Germany seems like one large garden. At first he is surprised by the tender care with which every corner of our country is planted and cared for, but then, as he ponders over the vastness of his own sparsely populated country, he realizes its youth as well as the fullness of his own life.

Probably the time has passed when, as Sombart expressed it, any American could "take flight into freedom," when vast sections of the West were still unopened, when, according to the homestead law, any settler could acquire 160 acres of land by a four years' residence. The Department of Agriculture reports that in those days the superabundance of land was the decisive factor in America's economic development. This land-wealth determined the mentality of the period. It molded the attitude of individuals and of the country as a whole towards economic problems. What a tremendous feeling of independence a man must have derived from the realization that he could build up a new life for himself and his family with the help of his own two hands. How stimulating to the spirit of adventure these conditions must have been! Now they have passed and the free land which is still available is too far away from the railroads and the necessary sources of supply. The original settlement of the country virtually came to an end in the nineties. Even in America the earth has almost all been given away.

America still possesses a magic charm, with the help of which an area of land, about the size of

Germany, can still be reclaimed. This charm, called irrigation, creates a new rich life in desolate prairies and in yellow desert sands.

Irrigation seems like a miracle when one travels from Kansas to the West. The fertile corn lands of the Mississippi Valley are followed by miles and miles of dreary desert where the aridity is so great that even grass turns yellow as early as May. At long intervals the train passes a farm where a few trees, planted near the house, show that a pathetic attempt has been made to indicate a human dwelling. Occasionally, from the train window, we noticed a few little towns, hot in the glaring sun. Then we passed another farm, a wooden house and some wooden sheds. The tools themselves stood in the open. Why should they not be left out of doors, when there is not the slightest chance that it will rain?

Suddenly and without knowing quite how we got there, we arrived in Denver. This city, with a population of 270,000, stands in the middle of this arid desert. Denver has prosperous industries and a flourishing trade, beautiful parks and avenues; there are flowers and lawns in front of the houses, which are not fenced off from the street. The land around this city is a strange sight: fields of wheat, alfalfa, or potatoes in the best condition, vegetable gardens and orchards and, in between these cultivated fields, expanses of arid soil where nothing grows, thus revealing that the cultivated parts have been reclaimed by irrigation. The water is brought from a stream in the mountains, and as this is not sufficient, a further water supply is transported in huge pipe canals from the other side of the mountains. Denver's prosperity is entirely due to irrigation. From above, the river is forced down to the valley through large irrigation canals, and then, later, smaller ditches carry the water to each separate farm. Artificial irrigation lakes retain the melted snow until the end of the summer. Up in the mountains the river is a large rushing torrent, but down in the valley it dwindles to a paltry stream. The river bed, dried up and covered with stones, merely indicates how the water will swell during the rainy season. When the summer is over, and Denver and the country around have been supplied with water, the river supply is always exhausted.

Every tree and every lawn in Denver has been artificially planted, nothing grew by itself. Farmers who did not contribute to the installation of the company, cannot obtain any water during dry periods when, as a result, their soil yields no crops.

This is Colorado, but California is even more magnificent. The country through which the railroad passes in New Mexico and Arizona looks more and more like a desert. With an average of 2.9 inhabitants to the square mile these two states are among the most thinly populated in the Union. At last nothing is visible in the yellow sand, where not even grass can grow, but cacti stretching their clusters of yellow flowers towards the blazing sun. On windy days clouds of dust sweep over the desert, threatening to choke out what little life remains. Then suddenly southern gardens seem to rise from the desert. The train passes vineyards and orange groves, planted in long straight rows of trees, which are all the same size. The yellow fruits shine forth among the dark green foliage. At first these orange groves are to be seen only at rare intervals as the train passes through long stretches of scrubby, unfertile country. Later, irrigated areas appear more and more often until the country looks like a glorious paradise, in which water and sunshine have been conjured up from the desert by some magic wand.

Fourteen million acres of land had been irrigated by 1909. During the next decade another five million acres were reclaimed and the present irrigation system is large enough to cover another seven million acres. According to recent estimates the territory already reclaimed (26 million acres) represents only half of the land in the United States which can be irrigated. The possible total is estimated at 51 million acres or about 20 million hectares. Irrigation is becoming more and more efficient, more technically perfect, all the time. It is true that in Colorado, where the irrigation ditches are still very primitive, a considerable part of the precious water evaporates or oozes away. It is estimated that approximately two-thirds of the water is wasted. In California, however, cement ditches and long pipe lines, extending through the entire cultivated area, have been laid and hydraulic pumps have been installed. In districts where this expensive system does not pay, dry farming is common. On these dry farms summer fallowing is practiced, the ground is plowed and kept free from crops for a season so that the moisture is retained in the soil for the coming year. The high costs of this method are somewhat counterbalanced by the fact that there is no danger of the harvests being spoiled by rain, and the soil is fertile under the sun.

So far, the land in America has not been fully exploited. In 1919 the 1903 million acres of land at America's disposal were used as follows: 483

million acres were covered with forest lands of which about half could also be used for pasture; dry pasture land and prairies showed an acreage of 587 million; 231 million acres were under grass; 122 million acres were covered by cities and roads or desert wastes; 480 million acres were covered by farm lands, though only 365 million acres had been tilled. The Department of Agriculture estimates that it would be technically possible to extend this area of arable soil to three times its present size, *i.e.,* to 973 million acres.

Current statistics indicate that all improved farm land is not actually in use. Farms are large in America and farm labor is scarce. For this reason the American farmer does not try to exploit every acre of his land. A German farmer wants to attain a maximum production per acre. The American farmer, on the other hand, like farmers in all colonial countries, only hopes that he will attain his maximum per capita production. If an American farmer has more land than he can operate, he lets a part of it "rest" for a year. The use of artificial fertilizers is relatively new in the United States, for hitherto there has not been much need for them.

Some of the mighty rivers in America, flowing with the lonely dignity of uncharted waters, are still unhampered, unrestrained by dams: there is so much land that it does not matter if some of it is occasionally flooded. In the same way unused farm lands can be seen again and again in America; soil which is waiting to be tilled by man.

Just now American agriculture is more concerned with reducing than with expanding its activities.

The worst depression [3] is past, but the effects of the war and the world-wide agricultural crisis are still being keenly felt in America.

The acreage of wheat increased from 47 to 75 million during the war. By 1924 it had dropped to 58 million, but this figure exceeded the pre-war acreage by about one quarter. America is still producing more wheat than can be sold to advantage. Central Europe's low purchasing power is exacting a heavy retribution from the farmer who realizes more poignantly than any one else in America to what an extent his own recovery depends upon the revival of Europe. The high food prices, which prevailed during the war, and the tremendous speculation in land which followed, resulted in equally high prices for land. Then came the depression. The average price for an acre of improved farm land throughout the United States rose from $58 in 1912 to $107 in 1920 and then fell to $78 in 1924. In Iowa, the richest agricultural State in the Union, these prices rose from $106 to $255 and then fell to $170. This price development, based on speculation, was accompanied by an enormous rise of mortgage debts. Mortgage debts per average acre in the United States rose from $9.99 in 1910 to $17.50 in 1920. In Iowa they rose from $26.63 to $63.19. Speculators

[3] Estimated value of farm products during the years in question (in millions of dollars):

	Crops	Animal Products	Total After Deduction of Crops Used for Fodder
1913 (pre-war production) ...	6,133	3,717	7,119
1919 (maximum post-war production)	15,423	8,364	17,810
1921 (depression)	6,934	5,468	9,922
1925 (revival)	9,953	6,111	12,204

who had borrowed every possible cent to buy land during the war were the first to feel the depression when it came. American agriculture as a whole suffered from the so-called "price scissors"; that is to say the disproportion between the prices of agricultural and industrial products. In his report for 1925 the Secretary of Agriculture complains that in fifteen wheat and corn growing states 8.5 per cent of the farmers surrendered their property to their creditors and that another 14.5 per cent actually went bankrupt. The Secretary reports also that in 1922 only 86.3 per cent of the livable farmhouses were occupied compared with 88.4 per cent in 1921 and 89.7 per cent in 1920. He reports that in 1922, 1,120,000 people, or almost 3.6 per cent of the rural population of the United States, migrated to the cities.

There are many causes for this emigration from the country. To a certain extent it reflects the increasing demand for industrial labor in the urban districts. Current restrictions on foreign immigration have caused American industry to fall back on the home labor reserve. Until 1920 wages for industrial and farm labor showed approximately the same development. According to the index numbers city wages were 226 per cent of the pre-war level while farm wages were 223 per cent. In 1922, however, industrial wages dropped to 201 per cent while farm wages fell as low as 139 per cent. The varying demand for both kinds of labor is reflected in these figures.

The migration to the cities also shows to what an extent improved machinery has decreased the demand for labor. The use of tractors, especially, has become more and more general during the last ten years. As a result the number of draught animals (*i.e.,* horses and donkeys; in America bullocks are never used to pull a plow) used by agriculture has declined to a marked degree. A corresponding decline in the number of farm hands has resulted.

The fact that the American farmer so frequently migrates from the land as soon as industrial conditions in the city warrant such a change is most characteristic of his mental attitude. Not only agricultural laborers are tempted by the higher wages they expect to receive in city factories. I was told at a large agricultural college, in an important agricultural state, that the attendance showed a marked decline during the recent agricultural crisis. Agriculture evidently did not appeal to farmers' sons, and this was not because they could not afford a college education. They went to college, but they took up engineering or some other profession. Why should they study agriculture when financially there is a greater future in something else?

It is the same old story: a farmer in America may be a farmer but he is also a business man. The fundamental difference between the farmer and the city dweller, as we Germans know it, does not exist in America. Nor is there such a marked difference in their modes of life, their outward appearance or their mental attitudes. An American farmer manages his farm as though it were a factory. He welcomes all technical improvements, when he believes that they pay in the end. Usually farms in America are specialized. There are few farms operated like the ones owned by German peasants where everything and anything is raised: cows, pigs, and chickens; fields planted with wheat, potatoes and fodder; a vegetable garden; a dairy department selling eggs, milk, butter and cheese. American farms usually stick to their specialty; there are cattle farms with corn fields, pig farms, wheat farms, chicken farms, fruit farms, etc. Sometimes specialization is carried so far that a farmer is obliged to purchase the foodstuffs he needs for his own household. An American farmer wants more than merely to earn his living (and by living he means an American standard of life). He wants to make money. He makes money from the farm when he can, or from some other enterprise, if this is easier. Above all he likes to make money by selling his farm, when this means an appreciable increase of his capital. Then he migrates, either to the city, or to some part of the country where agriculture is not so well developed or where the land is cheaper, and where, because of his experience, he can build up a new farm—and sell it again in the end. The love which the German peasant feels for his land, to which he clings tooth and nail for the sake of his children, is an attachment unknown to an efficient colonial (even if he is of German descent). In a state like Kansas, where the settlement began only seventy years ago, 2.5 per cent of the land changed hands annually during the last fourteen years. This means that since 1910 about a third of the farms in the state have passed from one owner to another. It should be noted, however, that these statistics include cases in which at the death of the father one son has bought his brothers' and sisters' share in the farm (children share an inheritance equally in America). But the census of 1920 shows that only 2,184,391, *i.e.*, only a third of the total 6,448,343 farms, had been operated by any one farmer for more than ten years. There were 1,086,485 farms, furthermore, which one farmer had operated for more than five and less than ten years. More than half of all the farms in the United States were not operated by the same person for more than five years. Conditions look somewhat more stable if farms operated by tenants are excluded, for tenant farms change hands even more frequently. But even among the 3,925,090 farms operated by owners in 1920 only 1,924,265, or about half, had belonged to the same farmer for ten years or more. During the fiscal year 1923-24 about 7 per cent of all the farms in the United States changed ownership and about 14 per cent of them changed managers. The rural population moves about as much as the urban population.

A knowledge of the distribution of property, therefore, is extremely important in judging the settlement of the land. At first sight this distribution is staggering (see table below). The total number of farms in the United States increased by 60 per cent during the last forty years. This rise really occurred during a thirty-year period ending in 1910, for after that, until 1920, the rise was relatively small. The number of owners operating these farms, however, increased only half as rapidly, namely by about 34 per cent. The number of tenants operating farms, on the other hand, was two and a half times as large as it was in 1880. In 1920 about 40 per cent of the farmers did not own the farms they operated, as compared with 25 per cent in 1880. (This last figure does not include actual farm labor.)

Year	All Farmers	Number of Farms Operated by				Per Thousand of Total Operated by Tenants
		Owners and Managers	Owners	Managers	Tenants	
1880	4,008,907	2,984,306	....	.....	1,024,601	256
1890	4,564,641	3,269,728	....	.....	1,294,913	284
1900	5,737,372	3,712,408	3,653,323	59,085	2,024,964	353
1910	6,361,502	4,006,826	3,948,722	48,104	2,354,676	370
1920	6,448,343	3,993,539	3,925,090⁴	68,449	2,454,804	381

It is a vital problem whether the broad masses of the rural population are already in a state of depressing dependence in this sparsely populated country which was settled such a relatively short time ago. The Departments of Agriculture and Commerce have studied this question intensively. For the following reasons their investigations were more optimistic than had been expected.

One and a half million of the total two and a half million tenants were operating farms situated in the South, where before the Civil War black slaves were used as farm labor. To-day 75.2 per cent of the Negroes working on farms are tenants as compared with 33.2 per cent of native born and 18.9 per cent of foreign born whites. These figures do not imply that Negro owners have lost their farms and become tenants. They signify rather that Negroes, who were once slaves, have risen to be tenants. This situation among the Negroes, and among some classes of whites in the South as well, does not imply a process of dispossession, but rather the development of a new relationship between owners and employees in the South.

The so-called "croppers," typical of conditions in the South, are in fact, all appearances to the contrary, nothing more than farm labor employed on a

⁴ 558,580 of these farms were owned only in part by the operator, who rented the rest of the land.

piece work basis. As a matter of fact it is more a juridical than an economic relationship: the large plantations in the South are subdivided into a number of small farms operated by these cropper tenants, who pay for their tenure in a fixed part of the crops produced. These croppers do not really operate their farms independently.

In other parts of the country, as well, tenancy is a means of attracting labor to the land. If this system were abolished these tenants would be replaced not by owners but by wage-earners who would be employed by the owner of the farm. Particularly in the South, therefore, a certain amount of permanent tenure exists. It is much less prevelant in the northern states.

It is the consensus of opinion "that, outside of the South, where the cropping system of tenancy largely prevails, especially among colored farm operators, there is no indication of the existence of any large body of farmers whose permanent status is that of tenants. On the contrary, the evidence seems to prove conclusively that tenancy is generally a convenient way of approach to full ownership. It is, in fact, a part of the agricultural ladder. Moreover, there has been no alarming increase in tenancy during the past two decades, and such increase as the figures show is mainly accounted for by the great appreciation in land values, which tends to lengthen somewhat the time necessary for the young farm tenant to accumulate savings for the purchase of a farm."

This ascent up the agricultural ladder is shown also by the ages of the various groups represented. The greater the age of a group of farm operators the smaller is the percentage of tenants and the larger the percentage of owners. In the first two age groups (under 25 and between 25 and 34) tenants predominate. In the first age group only 22.8 per cent own the farms they operate, in the second group 42.2 per cent are owners. In the higher age groups this relation of ownership and tenancy is completely reversed. Among farmers from 35 to 44 years of age the tenant percentage has declined to 39.8 per cent. In the next group only 20.7 per cent and 16.5 per cent, respectively, of the operators are tenants. As a rule young farmers are tenants. The older ones are owners. There is even more to the story. The older an operator grows the more he is able to pay off the mortgage debts of his farms. The majority of mortgage indebtedness is carried by young farmers. Of all farmers (including owners and tenants) between 45 and 54 years of age 69 per cent owned and 37.6 per cent were operating farms which were free from debt. The mortgage status among the farms operated by farmers in the next age groups is even more favorable when 51.2 per cent and 64.1 per cent, respectively, were free from debt.

This ladder is apparent even as the size of the property increases. Numerically the younger farmers predominate among farms of from 20 to 49 acres. Among men operating farms from 50 to 99 acres farmers between 35 and 40 years of age predominate. Numerically farmers between 45 and 54 predominate on the largest farms; the larger the farm the more the older age group predominates. These figures are all averages for the United States as a whole. When statistics for the South are excluded the picture looks even more favorable. Another statistical compilation, furthermore, shows to what an extent the American farmer can ascend the agricultural ladder. In the last census farm owners were asked whether they were originally tenants or wage earners before they bought a farm of their own. Answers from three and a half of the four million indicated that 34.7 per cent had begun farming as wage-earners, 43.3 per cent were originally tenants. By 1920 about 28 per cent of the operators, who had been tenants in 1910, owned their farms. Taking the normal death rate into account this percentage was as high as 33 per cent. If the South is excluded these percentages were 47 per cent and 53.6 per cent respectively. A number of investigations in specific districts emphasize this situation even more pointedly. In three Kansas townships (which are about the same as our village districts) 5.9 per cent of the present owners inherited their farms; 13.7 per cent acquired their property through the Homestead Act. The remaining 80.4 per cent bought their farms outright, and about three-quarters of these purchased their farms with an initial payment of 44 per cent. In five Illinois townships 15.5 per cent of the owners inherited their properties, whereas 69 per cent purchased them at an average initial payment of 27 per cent. The remaining 15.5 per cent bought their farms outright. The majority of these owners started as wage-earners. Some of them worked for a few years on their fathers' farms. Their savings made it possible for them to become tenants.

In the case of young men who stay on the home farm, the usual course is for the father, when the son marries, to establish him in business as a tenant. In other cases, after accumulating some capital out of their earnings, the young men start as tenants and aim to save enough to make the first payment on a farm, giving a mortgage for the balance. In the majority of cases these mortgages are slowly canceled, and the farmer reaches at an advanced period of life the status of an owner free from debt. The report of the Department of Commerce comes to the conclusion that tenancy in the United States, especially in the North, is largely a transitional status; that farm owners are constantly being recruited from the ranks of tenants and laborers; and that an agricultural career in the United States is essentially an economic ladder rather than a life of continuous endeavor on the same economic plane without opportunity to rise above the status in which one began . . . that the American farmer in a great majority of cases still spends the latter part of his life as an independent owner.

It is a decisive fact that America—except in the South—has developed no great landlordism which holds on tight and prevents newcomers from acquiring land. The colonial spirit of the northern states has always been opposed to a landed aristocracy, such as the one which burdens Europe in many forms. In the southern states, on the other hand, where large plantations and the slave traffic were the decisive factors, the European idea of a landed aristocracy was adopted. In America ownership of land does not imply social position, or social prestige. Agriculture is considered a business like any other. A farmer's financial success determines his social position. So far it is easier and takes less time to be successful in industry and trade than in agriculture. The incentive to build up large landed properties is therefore lacking. Throughout America the patrimony is divided equally among all the children. This fact would have made it difficult in any case to keep large estates intact. The operation of a farm with regular farm labor was difficult and uncertain, the chances of making profits, the opportunities for speculation, were not more tempting than they were in many other lines of business activity. Extensive speculation in land, which I have mentioned, is one reason why tenancy increased; the rent in such cases is relatively low because the speculator hopes eventually to make money on the land and in the meantime he wants to get some interest on his investment. Speculation in land is chiefly a local affair carried out by farmers themselves or by individuals who live in the neighboring towns. These people could just as well buy oil stocks; they are not interested in big long term land investments. Extensive domains, aside from public lands, are sometimes owned by railroad companies, to which they were granted when the railroad was being built. These companies try to settle their land, if it has increased in value sufficiently. Some timber and mining companies, as well, own large tracts of land, but these companies also sell it when the time seems favorable. These large estates are, therefore, no danger to society. The Department of Agriculture investigated the ownership of farm lands. This investigation showed that more than a third of the farm owners were still actively engaged in agriculture; approximately another third were retired farmers. The rest were chiefly country bankers, business men or professional people living in the country towns, who had either inherited a farm or acquired it by marriage, or had bought it as an investment or speculation. Fifteen per cent of the owners were women, usually the widows or daughters of deceased farmers. Absenteeism and the concentration of landed property are not entirely lacking, but so far they are limited. A great many of the tenants are simply sons or relatives of the owner, paying the interest and amortization out of the profits of their holding, and so gradually becoming owners themselves. The acquisition of a farm becomes more difficult as the higher price of the land and the enlargement of the equipment demands a greater capital.

The Commerce Department report closes by stating that "the idea of starting with nothing and making it into something was the typical idea of pioneer days. The original settlers in what is now the great agricultural section of the country took a piece of wilderness or prairie and made it into a farm; and for a generation or two the supply of new locations in the farther wilderness or the more distant prairie was such that the established farms did not attain a very great capital value, as compared with their annual production. But the pioneer days are now of the past; and the present-day idea is to take something of value and proceed to increase the value, or to make it productive of additional value."

The land wealth of the country is no longer as unlimited as it was when land was free for all. Now land has a market value, which has risen considerably. More capital is needed to-day to farm independently than was necessary ten years ago. It is easier for a farmer's son who inherits the land than for an outsider to acquire a farm. But still there is plenty of room for those who want to climb the agricultural ladder. Still there is freedom.

THE AMERICAN'S ENVIRONMENT

In the preceding chapters I have tried to give a picture of the American's environment. America's population has developed with a rapidity typical of colonial countries:

1850	23.19 millions
1870	38.56 "
1900	75.99 "
1910	91.97 "
1920	105.71 "
1925	113.49 "

This striking growth of the population continues despite immigration restrictions and birth control, but the increase is now less rapid than it was. For the decade ending in 1859 the increase was 35.6 per cent; for the decade ending 1910, 21 per cent; for that ending 1920, 14.9 per cent. For the five-year period ending in 1925 this rate of increase remained stable. The following table shows the urban and rural population of Continental United States (in millions):

	1900	1910	1920
Urban population	30.80	42.17	54.30
Rural population	45.20	49.81	51.41
Per cent urban of total ...	42.2%	45.8%	51.4%

These figures indicate that in the cities the population grew much more rapidly than in the country. From 1910 to 1920 the increase in the rural population was negligible. Besides, as I have mentioned

above, the crisis in 1921 caused a considerable emigration from the country districts. Up to 1910 the
combined population of American cities was increasing steadily but it was still less than the total rural
population. In 1920 the urban population, for the
first time, was bigger than the population in the
country. It should be noted in this connection that
among the rural population of 51.5 million only
31.61 millions were actively engaged in agriculture.

Do these figures imply a density of population in
relatively small urban districts despite the large area
of the country as a whole? It is true that in the
huge cities, of which I have written, people are
crowded together, but nevertheless statistics do not
imply the density of population which one would
assume if they were based on German or European
conditions.

For even in the large American cities a part of
the population lives in secluded country-like residential districts. For these people the city is only
the place where they work; they hardly even seek
their amusements in the town itself, much less do
they live there. In the smaller cities, on the other
hand, town and country life merge into one another
more and more. The statistics are really mislead-
ing, for they classify the inhabitants of cities having
a population of 2,500 and more as belonging to the
urban population. A great many of these small
towns, which can have a considerable population and
still be small, are not really urban, but country as
far as their life is concerned. Many of them are
located in huge monotonous prairies, and for miles
about there is no life except similar towns often
separated from them by considerable distances. In
these towns the little houses are surrounded by

fields, just like the farmhouses in the neighboring country. As a matter of fact there is not much difference between them and farmhouses, even in their outward form.

And this is the environment of a large part of America's population. The American can live in hope and freedom, but also in solitude, and in the void which he can fill or not, just as he pleases and just as far as he is able.

THE AMERICAN AND HIS AUTOMOBILE

This inner loneliness is hard to satisfy; it is easier to bury it beneath some superficial interest than it is to cure it fundamentally. The average American (like the average European of to-day), at any rate, finds it more convenient to hide this feeling of discontent under some outward activity. The rapid development of the automobile industry reflects this growing demand for an interest which will at least give him something to do. The gasoline consumed in the United States in 1923 amounted to 6,685 million gallons; that is 30,370 million hectoliters, or 275 liters per capita of the population. A little more gasoline was distributed, per capita, in America than beer was consumed in Bavaria, where the per capita consumption of beer in 1912 amounted to 238 liters, while the average German throughout the Reich as a whole was satisfied with 100 liters of liquid (beer not gasoline) per annum. The sale of books, both before the war and after, was smaller in both countries than the sale of beer or gasoline.

Automobiles have so completely changed the American's mode of life that to-day one can hardly imagine being without a car. It is difficult to remember what life was like before Mr. Ford began preaching his doctrine of salvation which made him the richest man in America. While I was in America I noticed huge dark-blue posters with white letters all over the continent: "Ford—seven thousand more since yesterday." This sign means that seven thousand Ford cars are manufactured and marketed

every day.   In addition to these Fords an almost
equal number of more comfortable, handsomer and
more expensive cars are produced every day.   These
are "real" cars, as they are called by people who
have risen above a Ford and whose successful self-
assurance is reflected in the kind of car they drive.
"Real" cars are sharply differentiated from Fords.
This whole development is the product of the last
fifteen, or indeed of the last ten years.   In 1910 only
181,000 passenger cars were produced in America,
and even in 1913 the figure was only 461,500.   By
1919 it rose to 1,657,652; in 1923, 3,485,298 cars
were produced annually.[5]

It is not easy for us to imagine the number of
passenger cars now in use in the United States.
Perhaps it is less difficult for us to grasp their value,
which is now estimated at 2,302.5 million dollars.
After deducting the value of exports (90.70 million
dollars) this figure indicates that the 110 to 113
million people living in the United States spent
9,290 million marks for passenger cars during one
year.   This sum includes only expenditures for new
cars; the upkeep of old ones is not considered here.
The 402,408 motor trucks, valued at 296 million
dollars, which were produced in 1923, are also a
separate item.

Besides, huge sums are spent every year by the

[5] In passing I should like to mention the number of telephones
in the United States. They numbered 237 million in 1902; 1,172
million in 1917; 1,435 million in 1922. Most recent statistics indicate that 19 per cent of the population in New York have a
telephone; in Chicago 23.8 per cent; in San Francisco 25.9 per
cent. In London, on the other hand, only 5.1 per cent of the
population have a telephone; in Paris 6.3 per cent; in Berlin
9.3 per cent. The rapid increase during the last few years of
the number of farmers having a telephone is of the greatest
importance.

Federal, State and Municipal Governments, for the upkeep and construction of automobile roads all over the country. It is already possible to travel from coast to coast by car, but soon the entire mileage, through deserts or across mountains, will consist of cement roads, wide and free from dust. Many such roads already exist. Along them filling stations, for refilling and repairing cars, have been installed by the large gasoline companies. Filling stations can be found everywhere in America. In large cities there are so many that, by car, they are only a few minutes apart. Even in prairie towns or mountain villages motorists are provided with gasoline stations.

Despite far-reaching traffic regulations automobile accidents occur frequently. A commission headed by the Secretary of Commerce, Herbert Hoover, reported that during 1923, 22,600 deaths and 678,-000 serious injuries, as well as a damage to property valued at 600 million dollars, were caused by accidents of various kinds, 85 per cent of which were automobile accidents. In 1924 automobile accidents were the cause of 450,000 injuries and 19,000 deaths. This means 52 deaths a day; 5,700 children were killed during the year in automobile accidents.

Every one concerned is making an effort to decrease this large number of casualties. Traffic regulations are being improved all the time. The public is constantly warned to be more careful. "A man was killed on this spot" a sign reads which is posted at many street corners in Chicago for the benefit of drivers and pedestrians. In the meantime, however, motor vehicles are rapidly becoming an independent means of transportation for passengers as well as for freight which is to be shipped short distances. Motor transportation is developing side by side with the railroad systems. Some of the railroad companies, in fact, are now using motor vehicles as public carriers on their side lines, so that the stations on their main lines can be decreased. This system saves labor and expenditures generally. According to one estimate, which may be slightly exaggerated, 17.73 million automobiles were being used in the United States in 1924. This would imply that every sixth American has a car, while all the rest of the world has only 3.63 million automobiles, or one-fifth as many cars as America has.

There are clever people in America who seriously assert that, economically speaking, the money spent for automobiles has not been a real expenditure. These people maintain that the saving of time, as well as the increase of efficiency resulting from the use of automobiles gives a prompt return for the money invested in cars. This is certainly not the case in downtown New York, where in the fantastically crowded ravine-like streets, there is hardly room for pedestrians, during rush hours, when the gigantic edifices swallow up or spit out their tens of thousands of employees. For automobiles there is no room at all at such times. Any one who is in a hurry must travel by subway in the bowels of the earth. In Chicago, however, where there is no subway, real American motor-car traffic can be observed. The streets leading to the residential districts are extremely wide, and before and after business hours the automobiles are crowded one after another along these streets. Two rows of cars, miles long, four cars broad on either side of the highway, move at the same orderly pace in opposite directions. One car follows the other in close succession until, out in the suburbs, this procession is broken up. New roads now being built in Chicago are wide enough to accommodate six cars side by side on both sides of the street. Some of these highways can accommodate as many as eight cars on either side; that is to say they are so wide that sixteen cars can be lined up on them. In the center of these roads there is a broad walk for pedestrians. Of course there are sidewalks on both sides as well. These broad highways are expected to accommodate the traffic for the next five years; it is not even hoped that they will be sufficiently wide after that.

On Sundays the motor traffic around the city is incredibly congested. A wise man starts on his drive at four o'clock in the morning, for so early in the day at least, the roads are relatively empty. Towards noon, however, the crush begins. Any one who is reckless enough to stay out late in the afternoon is lost in the maze of traffic, in an endless succession of cars. It is impossible to break through this line or to get ahead of the car in front, for every inch of the street is packed. On such Sunday afternoons it takes twice as long to get home as it did to drive out in the morning. Medium-sized cities are even more congested. During business hours the downtown streets are crowded with automobiles, which are lined up, one close to the other, at the side of the road. Half the street is taken up and it is quite a feat to squeeze in another car. Sometimes it is necessary to drive on for five or ten minutes before one can find a parking space. This delay is the only excuse for being late in America. At the same time it is in many cases an American city dweller's only chance to get some exercise. If he were not forced to walk from the place where he parked his car to his ultimate destination he would probably forget how to walk altogether. He always uses his car when he can. If there is enough room on the street to turn his car around he even drives from one block to the next.

For the farmer the automobile has been of the greatest practical importance. The motor car brought about a revolutionary change in his life. He is no longer isolated from the outside world, but is in constant contact with the city, and his mode of life is becoming more and more like that of a city dweller. Practically every farmer in America now has a car. Everywhere, even in the most isolated parts of the country, on the most primitive farms of the prairie or the desert, there is a car and a garage. I have been told that, not infrequently, when a man moves to a new farm, he packs his family and his belongings into his car, drives them to the site of land, and they live in the automobile until the new house is finished. The first thing he builds is the garage.

Now that he owns a car a farmer gets to town oftener, he talks with people more often, he sees and hears more of what is going on. It is now easy to associate with people living within a radius of fifty miles. He can belong to clubs and to other organizations which are equally far away from his farm. In the life of the American farmer the acquisition of a car, as well as of a radio, is extremely important. In cities a radio is only a new source of diversion, but on the farm it means far more. No matter how far away he is from the beaten path the farmer can keep in touch with market conditions, he hears the day's news promptly, and he can arrange his own business accordingly. Farm land, from which it formerly took days to reach the town, is now only a few hours away by car. This development has also increased the value of land. But the heightened value of life which has resulted from the use of cars, is even more important.

Automobiles have made life more worth while for Americans in general. With few exceptions they do not enjoy long out-door walks. They do not appreciate our German "Rücksack Idyll," either for their feet or for their backs. They play tennis or golf, but in these games the ball is more important than the sun. When the American does come face to face with the great natural beauties of his country— for if America lacks old cultural treasures she possesses in their stead the tremendous sights of Nature —his admiration is efficiently organized and made comfortable. Americans are massed into chars-à-bancs and are conducted through the beauties of nature according to a well-organized schedule. At certain points, when they are permitted to leave the char-à-bancs, the guide tells them that they may linger for ten minutes and exclaim "How pretty" and "Isn't that wonderful?" (Literally the guide says in his little speech: "This is Waterfall so-and-so, which is so-and-so many feet high. You may have ten minutes here but do not forget the number of your motor bus. This is motor bus No. 213.") In general the countryside is really too large for walking tours. Yellowstone Park, for instance, is one and an eighth times as large as the Free State of Hesse. Even in the most magnificent parts of the country one can ride for hours on end with no actual change of scene—everything is so broad, so expanded. It would be too trying and not really worth while to cover these distances on foot. It is only since he has acquired a car, therefore, that the American regularly explores the beauties of Nature. During the last ten years he has developed a real mode of outdoor life. The way in which he has taken up this new pastime is most illuminative of the sturdy boyish manner in which he goes at anything which interests him. This popularity of the outdoor life also illustrates how much Americans enjoy harmless pleasures.

All over the country Sunday is the great day on which to get out of doors. Cars are parked separately or in groups near the mountains, on the beaches, near rivers, lakes or woods. Tents are put up in front of the cars and the picnickers sit around them resting, cooking or playing. They wear the simplest sport clothes: men, women and children often wear the same kind of practical overalls when they drive out into the country on a Saturday afternoon. When they find a spot which they like they spend the night in their tent. They bring cooking utensils and plenty of food in the car quite comfortably. If they feel like it they move on to another place which appeals to them more. They spend Saturday afternoon and Sunday out of doors in the fresh air; it is a healthy, inexpensive and enjoyable pastime. Not only week-ends are spent this way. More and more Americans are using their cars for their summer vacations. This is all the more important, because, as a rule, vacations in America are shorter than they are in Germany. In large business concerns the employees, as well as the director, as a rule, have only a two weeks' holiday. Higher placed employees can be away longer but they must take leave without pay. I was told that as a matter of fact many American men do not really like to interrupt their work for more than two weeks. Among families who are well off, it used to be customary for the wife and children to stay in the country longer, while the husband remained in the city to go on making money. These automobile trips (the man, of course, drives himself and many women, too, drive their own cars) bring families more closely together on their vacations.

The increasing popularity of these outings spent in the car has brought about all kinds of conveniences. Parking space has been provided, for insofar as the land is not public property it belongs to private individuals, and cannot be used without some special arrangement. Besides, cleanliness and a certain amount of comfort are necessary for longer trips. Americans are used to these advantages, and to do without them would be considered unhygienic and would spoil their pleasure. Aside from fresh drinking water, sanitary toilets and baths or shower baths are needed, and one must be able to wash clothing. Gas for cooking is also wanted when it can possibly be arranged, as well as electric light.

Throughout the country there are camps of all kinds. Some of them are run by the owners of filling stations, who sell food and drink in small quantities, and provide wooden tables and running water. Some of these camps, however, which are maintained by municipalities or forest administrations, are less primitive and provide all the conveniences mentioned above. The purpose of these automobile trips is not only to enjoy the beauties of Nature; people want to see the cities they drive through as well. For this reason a number of municipalities have installed camps on the outskirts of the cities.

These beautiful camps are not only fitted out with all the conveniences necessary to comfort: wooden shacks or tents are provided as well, in which the tourist can live. These camps near the cities are gay, airy places, which are always invitingly clean and comfortable, and it costs nothing or very little to use them. It goes without saying that these camps compete with the hotels situated in the city itself, but the tourists do not want to spend money on hotels. The cities are interested in encouraging motorists, from whom they derive some benefit in any case. Above all the people themselves demand the opportunity of camping out, and of enjoying this inexpensive and informal way of traveling.

In America such an effort is being made to meet this demand that in the great National Parks, which were visited by more than six million people altogether in 1923, besides the luxurious hotels, there are camps for tourists, who, because of the great distance involved, have come by train and not by car. In these camps are simple but immaculately clean tents. Meals are excellent but inexpensive. In the evenings there is music while one sits around the camp fire, and dancing in a large wooden hall. A German might think that he had come upon a camp maintained by the Youth Movement, but as a matter of fact these campers are of all ages, classes and incomes. They have all left their formality and seriousness at home and have come out to have a harmless good time. Every one feels the same self-assurance, he is just as much a part of the whole as every one else; every one is considerate of his neighbors in this democratic camp community where all class differences disappear. Every camper is at home and no one feels out of place.

"The automobile," Secretary Hoover declared in a recent speech, "is no longer a luxury, it is a complete necessity. It has added *recreation, efficiency* and *vision* to the American people. Probably 75 per cent of our people participate in its use." These three words cannot be expressed in German, but the reader will doubtless feel their pregnancy and significance.

There is no question but that the automobile is another expression of the American's inner restlessness. He always wants to be doing something and he wants to accomplish everything, even his leisure and his pleasure, in a hurry. Many who have spent the day driving have nothing to tell the next morning except how many miles they covered. But for the majority of people living in this peculiar country with its peculiar housing facilities, a car does mean greater freedom. I was told in California that in the spring of 1925, 200,000 workers and their families were living in out-of-door camps; after losing their jobs in the East they had packed up everything they owned and had migrated to the West to find work. They would never have been able to afford the expensive trip by rail, but traveling in their cars they were able to pick up enough odd jobs on the journey to pay their way. Even migratory workers, whose wretched existence consists in traveling around this enormous country for months so as to be wherever crops are being harvested, often use an automobile for their journey. Any one meeting a group of these migratory workers anywhere would think he had chanced upon gypsies.

Aside from these specific cases the automobile has enormously enriched the life of the American people as a whole. It means a great liberation not to be bound to any one spot in this vast and lonely country (even if a car only takes one to another place which is equally lonely). To be able to move about freely, to be independent of railways with their bothersome time-tables, tickets, and crowds, means greater freedom.

For this reason the American simply must have his car. If he cannot afford an expensive one he wants a Ford at least. If he cannot afford a new Ford, which costs three or four hundred dollars, he buys one of the used ones which are offered for sale everywhere. There are the funniest, strangest old cars in America, especially among the students who consider it particularly smart to drive a car when there is nothing left of it but the wheels and the frame.

The will to possess a car is like the will to possess a house, except that this desire for a car, which is less expensive than a house, is usually more easily satisfied. At any rate both desires are an incentive to hard work; they give an aim and an ambition which the majority of people in America can realize. Cars and houses are, therefore, really in the center of the American economic system, of the American economic will.

And is not this a magnificently clever trick on the part of this system? Who can tell what might have become the great aim of masses of the population, how their attitude towards the state and towards society might have developed, if this economic system itself had not been able to offer them material aims, which are near at hand and so relatively easy to reach? Twenty years ago silk stockings were jestingly called the bait of the American economic system. Now it is cars and houses. Ford seems to think that airplanes will be next. He is making his preparations for this stage of development. I shall later refer again to the influence of these facts on the American's social consciousness. At any rate it is true that in America the automobile already belongs to the people. The average, according to which every sixth American has a car, may be somewhat exaggerated. In the first place the number of cars actually in use is probably not as great, and in the second place families owning two or three cars are of course included in this average so that there are more families without any car at all than might appear at first. It is, however, a fact that a considerable proportion of American wage-earners already own a car and the rest believe that they, too, will one day possess one. This is the second great symbol of American prosperity.

THE ACCESSIBILITY OF EDUCATION

THROUGHOUT America, side by side with the uproar and confusion of gigantic cities, or in the monotonous loneliness of isolated country towns and solitary farms, there is an astonishing number of districts which seem to belong to a world other than this European-colonial, modern-capitalistic, technically-developed country. These districts seem like enchanted islands of another century, islands made for leisure, concentration and the development of youth.

These are the colleges and the universities and their campus grounds. There are wide lawns for every kind of sport or game and broad avenues planted with trees which curve together at the top like the arch of a cathedral. The college buildings, standing together on this large plot of ground, seem like a little city: classrooms and seminars and college halls, institutes of various kinds, and libraries which are often astonishingly large, churches and chapels, administration buildings, clubs for the professors, and for the men and women students. In some cases these clubs are connected with a students' coöperative store. Then there are dormitories, numerous fraternity houses, where some of the members live, gymnasiums with swimming pools, etc.

Many of the eastern colleges resemble in architecture Oxford University. At these eastern colleges, such as Princeton, an old and distinguished institution, ivy-clad gothic predominates; there are green enclosed courtyards and cross-arched vaults. The common dining-halls are high and festive, like churches, with stained glass windows and carved woodwork. Leland Stanford, a young university in California, two "automobile hours" from San Francisco, on the other hand, is built in the old Spanish mission style. The buildings are light and colored and joyous, and fit in with the brilliant sun and abundance of flowers and the gorgeous vegetation generally. Many of the other universities were not built according to any historical style of architecture, but almost all of them are architectural units and consistent; they are beautiful, spacious, purposeful and in good taste. Columbia University, in New York, is the only university I saw which, because of a lack of space, has no campus, and which, like the rest of the city, was forced to expand skyward. Nevertheless Columbia, with the massive solemnity of its buildings covering a large plot of ground, offers a picture of powerful, impressive energy.

The inside of these buildings is correspondingly impressive. In all of the common rooms, especially the libraries, clubs and dining halls, there is an amplitude of comfort, a luxurious ease of rocking chairs and armchairs. The halls for sports, games, and dancing are so lavishly expansive that one seems to sense a conscious effort to serve a definite end.

What is the significance of this effort to surround the students with beauty and the culture of wealth, especially when most of them come from and will later return to homes which are very simple and quite different from these university surroundings? Or have these surroundings been created by plutocratic parents who hope to rear their sons and daughters to an aristocratic consciousness? Is it perhaps that this colonial country, which lacks an aristocracy of birth and has so far developed no landed aristocracy, is hopeful that it may, under the influence of such plutocratic environment at the universities, evolve an aristocracy based on the privilege of education? Do these universities aim to teach the students to consider themselves as privileged beings as a result of the privileges and traditions they enjoyed at these institutions, just as the Reserve Officers' class in pre-war Germany was based on the privileges and traditions of the officers' casinos?

There are isolated cases in which these motives play a certain part. There are colleges, supported by wealthy private foundations, which admit only a very limited number of students and are as exclusive as private schools. There are fastidious fraternities with very good "connections," which pave the way for their members to obtain important Government jobs. In the East there are a few world-famous institutions, conferring degrees that are like titles of nobility in this country where nobility and titles do not exist. A degree from these institutions can, however, only be secured by merit.

But most of the universities are not built so luxuriously and are not trying either to develop an exclusive group of educated individuals or to accustom them to a luxurious, exclusive mode of life. On the contrary, the universities are made as universally attractive as possible so that more and more people in this colonial country will be tempted to get a higher education. Many of these institutions are maintained by private endowments. Contributions from the alumni flow constantly into the treasuries. The donors take great pride in their own generosity which they really consider as a monument to themselves.

State Universities are similarly well equipped. A colonial country, with no history, is proud to be able to offer its youth these advantages. The State of Wisconsin spends about three-quarters of its total income on roads (chiefly for the benefit of motorists) and on education. That is a typical example.

It is a decisive fact in America that the privileges of education are not monopolized by property. No matter how great the extraordinarily far-reaching power of plutocracy may be in this democratic country, the accessibility of education is not conditioned by wealth or lack of wealth. Any one can have a higher education who is willing to fight for it. For the road, leading towards this education, is open to all. It is uniform and broad and becomes narrower at the top. On this road, aside from the opportunities for learning, there are possibilities of finding the means to make a higher education possible.

Grammar school, high school, college, university; these are the mile-stones of the education which is open to all. To understand this educational system one must realize first of all that the aim of education is not the same in America as it is in Germany. People who know America well agree in this. They believe that in America the practical aim is the ruling factor throughout, from the first day in the grammar school to graduation from a university. The chief function of education in America is to equip young people with the practical knowledge they will need later, and to teach them how to be able to cope with life, which is a struggle. It is grotesque when this idea is carried out in so-called military academies, which have nothing in common with the

army or the navy except that the students and instructors run around in semi-military uniforms, and
that the whole atmosphere in these boarding schools
is based on military drill and discipline. Training
itself is everything in these schools, lessons must be
prepared in a large common hall: for later when the
boys are in business they will be obliged to work in
huge offices, with hundreds of people pounding typewriters all around them; they will be forced to answer the telephone, to receive visitors and to take
part in conferences in crowded rooms. Therefore
it is considered advisable for them to acquire the
necessary concentration when they are children.
This is an extreme case, but even in regular schools
it is not knowledge, and much less any depth of
knowledge, which counts; the chief aim is to teach
children how to apply their knowledge practically
and sytematically. This is the ideal of the American
educational system, through high school and college,
which is a cross between the last years at our
"gymnasia" and the first terms at our universities.
Graduate schools at the universities offer specialized
training for people who want to teach later on themselves, or who want to take up a practical professional career. There are also specialized institutes
for the training of physicians, lawyers and other
professions. "To the average, intelligent American," Ludwig Lewisohn writes in "Up Stream,"
"education, for which he is willing to deny himself
and pay taxes, means skill, information—at most,
accomplishment. Skill and knowledge with which
to conquer the world of matter. Our students, then,
came to the university not to find truth, but to be
engineers or farmers, doctors or teachers. They
did not want to be different men and women. So

let me repeat: Our people do not believe in education at all—if education means a liberation of the mind or a heightened consciousness of the historic culture of mankind. College is to fit you to do things—build bridges, cure diseases, teach French. It is not supposed to help you to be."

A number of professors in many universities and colleges told me the same story. There are a few exclusive institutions which cultivate knowledge for knowledge's sake the way we do, but most of them aim chiefly to supply practical information for the practical professions, in which the students are interested. In the great majority of universities economics is taught from the business point of view. Instructors in Germany, who are teaching practical economics, would be thrilled if they knew how comprehensibly their subjects are being taught in America; they have no idea how extensive their field really is. One of the subjects most popular among women students is called Home Economics. In these courses the young women learn how to manage a household efficiently; they are taught how to buy household goods, how to economize, how to cook, how to set a table; they learn all about dietetics. After college these women become home economics instructors, managers of hospitals, laboratory assistants, etc. Physical training is an important factor in American education. During the first two years of college some sport is obligatory for men and women students. Sometimes the young men have regular military training. In the gymnasium of a large agricultural college I saw rows of guns and in the courtyard outside regular military drill was going on. It was not some military camp, as I thought at first, but a regular part of the col-

lege curriculum. I saw the same thing again at
other universities during my stay in America. The
War Department assigns officers to the universities,
where they become regular members of the faculty.
Next to this physical training, specialized courses,
which will equip the students to take up some specific profession, are most important.

Some of the students come to college to supple-
ment their high school education and to enjoy a
carefree life for a while. They also hope to form
associations, to make connections, which will be useful to them later when they are in business. Not a
small proportion of the women students hope to
make connections in college which may lead to marriage. Sometimes the instructors make greater demands on the students in the hope of raising the
academic standard of the institution. It is not impossible in such cases that the students may object
on the grounds that this is not what a college is for.
If, however, the instructors insist on their point of
view during the examinations, and "flunk" a large
number of students, it is not impossible that the
board of trustees may object on the grounds that it
is the function of the university to pass students,
and not to send the greater part away. For colleges
and universities in America are not independent,
self-administering organizations as they are in Germany. They are administered, like a business organization, by a board of trustees consisting of men
who support them financially, or appointed by the
governor of the state. He or these trustees appoint
the president, who is rarely a scholar, and more
often a practical administrator, who knows how to
conduct the extensive business of the institution,
how to manage the building operations which are

being carried out, how to administer the finances. The instructors, on the other hand, are employees, officials in this administrative system. Where business interests are involved, there is a considerable possibility of friction in this type of university administration. Instructors are very frequently the weaker contenders in such conflicts. Socialistic instructors are unpopular. Any one who is not entirely enthusiastic about the prevailing system may easily be labeled a socialist in America; that is, unless the public verdict of the interested parties (like similar verdicts in some parts of Europe) tries to damn this trouble-maker irrevocably by simply calling him a bolshevik.

All this must be taken into consideration in connection with American universities, or one might think that America is about to become a republic consisting only of scholars. Education in America means above all training for some practical profession. This point cannot be emphasized too often. But even so it is of a high social significance that American education is not a privilege of certain classes only. It is the great principle of American democracy to let every one mold his own life, to give every one the same opportunity. No matter to what an extent this principle is dropped when people are older (when the unequal distribution of property implies great advantages for the few and great disadvantages for the many) when Americans are young they can overcome these differences if they have ability. In the grammar school, which corresponds to our "Völkschule," the selective process begins. A bright child can progress more quickly, the less capable pupil falls behind. In the high school, elective courses offer clever students greater

possibilities to get ahead, and eliminate less profi-
cient boys and girls, who can continue in private
schools, if they wish, for the public schools in any
case do not bother with them any more. Graduation from high school is necessary before entering
college. Grammar school, high school and college
(as far as it is a state institution) all are free. Even
educational appliances are given to the pupils. In
the state university, students who are citizens of the
state pay no tuition at all, or only a small entrance
fee of a few dollars. Thus this democratic country
is doing its share in making education accessible to
all, regardless of who and what they are. Economic
prosperity and the open mindedness of society are
doing the rest to enable these young people to take
advantage of these opportunities. These two factors make it possible for capable students to work
their way through college. If necessary they can
even do without financial help from their parents.

To avoid misunderstanding I should like to state
that not every young American goes to college. The
poorest, whom economic pressure at home robs of
their freedom, are hardly able to do so. Great de-
termination and will-power on the part of the parents as well as the children would be necessary in
such cases to send a boy or girl to college. In the
lowest stratum of American society this will-power
is still frequently lacking. In this stratum masses
of children are burdened so young with outside
work, that when they leave school they have completed only a few years of actual schooling, and the
idea of the accessibility of education has never been
awakened in them. Often they are forced to become

wage-earners at such a tender age that their will is broken.

Child labor is one of the most malignant growths infesting American society. Progressive people, especially women, are working with all their power against this exploitation of children. Progressive newspapers frequently publish drawings showing a child at a cross-road: one path leads to a school, the other to a factory. Hundreds of thousands of very young American children, even to-day, take the road which leads not to the school but to the factory, just as was the case in Europe during the worst period of early capitalism. A number of states have tried to protect children by law against this exploitation. But no matter to what extent the child's welfare may be the center of interest in other phases of American life, so far, despite many efforts, no Federal law has emerged making child labor illegal. Twice Congress passed such a law, but both times the Supreme Court declared it to be unconstitutional. Sponsors of child-labor legislation then tried to pass taxation measures, according to which products made with child labor were to be heavily taxed, but again these measures were declared to be unconstitutional. To make state child-labor legislation effective, an attempt was made to prohibit interstate commerce in commodities produced by child labor, but this, too, was declared to be unconstitutional. The fight for the emancipation of the child from this slavery is going on despite these defeats and an encouraging partial success has been achieved in various states. In the Federal Government, however, and only Federal legislation would have any far-reaching effect, any attempts to abolish child labor have failed because of the opposition to such a "curtailment of liberty."

And yet how strangely things overlap in America. In several cities I noticed boys in the higher grades of the grammar schools, sons of well-to-do parents, who spent a few hours Saturday mornings working in some shop, or some business enterprise, or somewhere else, wherever they found an opportunity to earn some money. This is not an exploitation of children. It is really a supplementary education, teaching them, while they are young, how to deal with practical problems. This practice is quite in accord with the educational ideal and the spirit of the country. In the high schools this practice is even more general. If a student must earn his own living, he can do so outside of school hours. In the colleges and the universities many students accept it as a matter of course that they shall earn their own living. Some students at a western university happened to see a report about the German "Werkstudenten" (students working their way through college) in which this post-war development at German universities was described with great enthusiasm. The American students, however, shook their heads. "It is very nice," they said, "that German students have gradually progressed to this extent, but with us it was always customary to earn our own living. Why should any one write books about it?"

And it is a fact that a large proportion of American students, either at the state universities or at endowed institutions, where the expensive tuition makes it all the more necessary, are working their way through college, either entirely or in part. It is this practice which makes it possible for such masses of the population to go to college. This is liberty indeed, and it takes freedom from prejudice, the democratic respect for all honest work, to create such a spirit. For if a young man or a young woman hopes to find an opportunity for work in an institution which is far away from any large city, he or she must be willing to perform any kind of labor, no matter how humble. College girls are often helpers in a household. In San Francisco, for instance, they get their room and board for two hours' work a day. If they work a few hours more on Saturdays, they get from ten to fifteen dollars a month in addition, which gives them their pocket money. Men students, also, do hard work in the household (cleaning windows and floors) for from 35 to 50 cents an hour. Or they are waiters in restaurants. Please consider: they wait on tables in restaurants frequented by their professors and their fellow students, by whom they are considered and treated like gentlemen in spite of—or perhaps just because of—their work. Or they act as salesmen in shops, they are typists or bookkeepers in some business or library, where they work on an hourly basis. Some of them are gardeners on the campus, others are employed by a laundry, and they collect the laundry and return it when it is finished. In America there are many possibilities for people who are not afraid of work. When these students are older and have acquired a little knowledge it is even easier. During their vacation they act as assistants to engineers or farmers, whichever they hope one day to be themselves. Or they are chauffeurs or waiters, or porters in a hotel or a camp in some summer resort or national park. During the university vacation one never knows in these resorts whether the young man driving the car or carrying the luggage is not a future doctor of philosophy, or whether the waitress is not a future woman physician. But it makes no difference, for the elevator boy and the waitress are respected in this country in any case. Even if they are not disguised students, they have the natural self-assurance characteristic of a free people.

Much is still in the process of evolution, in the beginning, as it were, but it is most significant how quickly the use of this freedom is developing. Statistics concerning the attendance at colleges and universities—exclusive of the large number of extension course institutions of various kinds—show the following development during the last two decades.

	1900–01	*1910–11*	*1921–22*
Male	75,472	119,026	269,560
Female	38,900	64,546	168,262
	114,372	183,572	437,822

These figures seem even more striking if they are compared with general population statistics, which show that in the decade ending in 1910 the population as a whole increased by 21 per cent, whereas the number of students increased by 60 per cent. During the next eleven years the population as a whole increased by 17 per cent, the number of students by 138 per cent. These figures indicate the youth of this movement and indicate how rapidly it is developing. In certain states, with Wisconsin leading, the aim seems to be approaching its goal; that ultimately the entire youth of the country, all the boys and girls, will go through college. The time will come when college-trained workers will run the machinery in the factories. This optimism for the future is already reflected in the vitality of the American people. A young American woman, traveling in Germany, asked a thirteen-year-old boy what he intended to do when he had finished school. "I want to be a cook," he told her. The American girl could hardly get over her surprise: an American lad of the same age would have said, at least, that he wanted to "become a millionaire," and probably he would have announced his intention of becoming "President of the United States."

The various states of the Union are making every effort to develop their educational systems. The number of illiterates is still extremely large, despite the fact that primary education has been compulsory for a long time. The country is too large, and the people living in it represent too many races and modes of life, to overcome illiteracy very quickly. It is hoped that the automobile will help in this problem to a certain extent. In many parts of America small country schools are now being replaced by centralized district schools, grammar and high schools, so that the rural population can have access to the same education provided for people in the cities. In motor buses children from the districts all around are called for and are taken home again when school is over for the day. Besides, there is the increasing demand for a college education. This desire is now so strong that older people who are beginning to feel the competition of college-trained youth, are trying to increase their knowledge through correspondence courses, which are maintained by special departments in many universities and by a number of private correspondence schools as well. Difficult and full of problems as this method may be, it has nevertheless developed tremendously in America. Pioneer days, when bank directors and railway presidents began their career as messenger boys, and when every messenger hoped one day to be President, are drawing to a close in America. A college education is more and more becoming a prerequisite for advanced jobs, even in business. Here and there the standards of the universities themselves are becoming more exacting. To enter the famous Harvard Law School, for instance, a college degree is now required. Night schools, which make it possible to study law in the evening after a day's work, are being more and more curtailed, and with them the chance for eager lawyers to make money. The differences in educational standards are growing more stable, as education as a whole is improving. But as long as education is not a hereditary privilege of certain classes these differences imply no hereditarily fixed class differences. The fact that America has been able to maintain a free educational system, which is accessible to all, despite the increasing demand for education, seems to me to be the third symbol of American prosperity.

FIGURES OF PROSPERITY

THE figures quoted in this chapter will, I think, reëmphasize America's great prosperity, three symbols of which—housing conditions, automobiles and the accessibility of education, I have already discussed.

The United States, with about one-sixteenth of the total world population, produces about three-quarters of the total world production of petroleum and about three-fifths of the total iron production. The United States produces more than half of the total world production of cotton and copper; it produces about two-fifths of the total world production of coal and lead; and as much as a quarter of the world production of wheat. By 1921 two-fifths of the world's total water power was produced in the United States, where the exploitation of water power is still going on rapidly. These few instances will indicate how lavishly nature has provided for Americans; the rest they have achieved themselves through hard work. As early as 1912 the national wealth was estimated at 186.30 billion dollars—Helfferich's estimate of Germany's national wealth in 1913 was 73.80 billion dollars. In 1922 the national wealth of the United States was estimated at 320.80 billion dollars. The average per capita wealth in Germany, in 1913, before the devastating effects of the war, was $1,107. In America, on the other hand, the average per capita wealth in 1912 was $1,950, and in the year 1922 it amounted to $2,918.

The dollar inflation (illustrated by the fact that

the Wholesale Index, 1913 = 100, was 149 in 1922)
must, of course, be considered, but the increase of
the national wealth at a time when Europe was
growing steadily poorer, was nevertheless so marked
that, despite a simultaneous increase in the population, the real value of the per capita wealth remained
unchanged. It should, however, be remembered in
this connection that for the United States the war
did not result in war profits only, enormous as they
may have been, for at the same time America was
granting loans to the allies and was spending large
amounts herself for war purposes, so that she was
assuming tremendous debts, which are now being re-
deemed. It should also be remembered that American citizens, especially those who were wealthy, were
taxed very heavily because of America's participation in the war. Incomes of less than $2,000 were
free from taxes, but the large incomes were taxed
up to 60 per cent. Unless incomes were invested
in certain securities, which were declared by law to
be free of taxation in any case, it is held by experts
that most people in America paid their taxes con-
scientiously. The publicity given to income tax dec-
larations probably encouraged such prompt payment.
The National Industrial Conference Board estimates
total tax payments during the height of the deflation
crisis (1921) at 8,363 million dollars (as against
2,194 million in 1913). In 1921, according to the
National Industrial Conference Board, these taxes
constituted about 16.7 per cent of the total national
income. In 1923 the Board estimated them at 7,716
million, which, according to the Board, represented
11.5 per cent of the national income. These figures
would indicate that the financial burdens which
America assumed during the war were not incon-

siderable. The difference is, however, that while Europe is still struggling through her period of reconstruction, America has already overcome this difficult stage, and is beginning to increase her wealth as a whole.

National income statistics indicate this revival. In 1913 the total national income of the United States was estimated at 34.4 billion dollars, which meant a per capita income of $354.00 as compared with a per capita income of $243.00 in England and $146.00 in Germany in the same year.

In 1918 the American national income amounted to 61 billion dollars, the average per capita income was $586.00. If the decline in the purchasing power of the dollar is considered in this connection the real value of the national income in 1918 amounted to 38.8 billion dollars, the real value of the per capita income to $372.00. These figures indicate, therefore, that even towards the end of the war the national income showed an increase as compared with 1913. Since the end of the war this increase has continued.

From 1918 to 1923 the Wholesale Price Index fell from 194 to 154 (in 1920 it had risen to 226). In the meantime the national income had risen to 67 billion dollars in 1918, which meant an increase by 10 per cent over 1913. It is not necessary in this connection to mention the difficulties connected with such estimates of a country's national wealth and income. These American figures emphasize an upward trend too clearly to leave room for any doubt as to the country's general prosperity.

It is a fact of the utmost importance that labor, too, is participating in this general prosperity. In preceding chapters I have described the outward manifestations of this development, which is also proven by statistical figures.

It is a well-known fact that nominal wages are much higher in the United States than they are in Germany. Roughly estimated, average American wages are four or five times higher than German wages. The hourly wage of an unskilled worker in Ford's plant was in the summer of 1925 75 cents; his earnings for an eight-hour day therefore amounted to $6.00 a day. Hourly wages for skilled workers average $1.25, *i.e.*, $10.00 a day.

Wages for unskilled workers as a whole are not as high as they are in the Ford factory. I was told that in the Pittsburgh steel industry, for instance, unskilled workers earn 50 cents an hour, *i.e.*, $4.00 a day. In other industries the wage level for unskilled labor is even lower, especially as far as women workers or children are concerned. The latter are frequently exploited to a very terrible extent.

Wages for highly skilled labor, on the other hand, are often higher than those paid in Detroit, particularly in the building trades, where for certain jobs wages are as high as $12.00 a day. It should be borne in mind, however, that many of these highly paid trades are purely seasonal occupations or trades which depend very largely on business cycles. In any comparison with European conditions the difference in the purchasing power of wages in America and Europe, as well as the difference due to the system of social insurance which increases a German workman's real wage, should be remembered. It is difficult to compare the purchasing powers of the dollar and the mark, but in general the real value of the dollar is estimated at about half its nominal value, so that the purchasing power of a dollar is assumed to be the same as that of two marks. Judging by my own impressions, however (and I realize, of course, that they can have been only fragmentary), I should say that this comparison may, perhaps, be too unfavorable for American currency; that is to say, a dollar may really be worth more in actual purchasing power than two marks. For foodstuffs are relatively cheap; in many cases they are only a little more expensive than they are in Germany. The various commodities, which are manufactured wholesale for everyday use, are not appreciably more expensive than they are in Germany. Rent is very high, but it should be borne in mind that the more prosperous wage-earners in America have houses which are far better than the average dwelling of a German worker. All American products which require considerable labor in their manufacture, are very expensive in America. Prices for luxury products are particularly high. Even if in comparisons of living standards the real value of the dollar, as compared with the mark, is assumed to be half its nominal value, it is a fact that the living standards of the American wage-earner are twice or two and a half times as high as the living standards of German workers. High standards of life have become general in America since the war, where not only nominal wages but these standards have been raised as well.

In this connection the National Industrial Conference Board has made some interesting investigations, covering twenty-three industries, which include about 16 per cent of all the American wage-earners employed in industry. The average length of the working week among these wage-earners decreased from 51.5 to 48.2 hours from 1914 to 1924.

Despite this decrease in hours average weekly wages increased from $12.54 to $26.94, *i.e.*, by 115 per cent, during this decade. It should be mentioned that the cost of living index rose from 100 to 165.6 during this period. But, despite this rise, the real weekly wage—according to this study—nevertheless increased by 31 per cent. The statistics compiled by this employers' association have not remained unquestioned, but even if some reductions may be necessary, there remains for the country as a whole a distinct curve of prosperity.

II. THE AMERICAN ECONOMIC SYSTEM

THREE ECONOMIC AREAS

Spaciousness is the ruling symbol of American life: spaciousness, loneliness and emptiness. The area covered by the United States is nineteen times as large as Germany, but the number of people living in this area, which includes the greater part of the American Continent, is not quite twice as large as the population of Germany. In Germany 328 individuals, on an average, inhabit a square mile; in the United States, on the other hand, the density is only 35.5. The German people, however, are confined to one-ninth the area inhabited by Americans who can, and do, move about freely. This fact symbolizes the fundamental contrast between life in the Old World and in the New.

This spaciousness directs and controls America's economic development. A European, especially if he has been in the United States himself, and has seen only New York or one or two other large cities in the East, may easily consider American economic life in terms of unchangeable formulæ. He may think of trusts and Wall Street, the tremendous business activities dependent upon these institutions. Once he associated them in his mind with American competition, now he associates them with American capital and American credits, both of which are eagerly sought after by Europe.

An American considering his country's economic development has quite a different point of view from the European's. An American thinks of his country's soil, he realizes that it is as large as all of

Europe put together, even including Russia, which, before the war, constituted six-tenths of the entire European area. He thinks of the United States as one country, as one economic kingdom, as it were, where there are no differences of nationality, no differentiations in the commodities consumed by the population in the various districts. There are no tariff walls, no language barriers, the currency is the same all over the country. There are no passport difficulties though one travel from one end of the continent to the other. The railroad systems are inter-connected, and the highways are connected and coördinated. The American thinks of his country as that part of the world which is subject to his will, as a unified market which can absorb his own products. An American, who is in business or finance, or who is interested in the country's economic development generally, thinks of this soil primarily as a great field for his activities, as that part of the world where he can express himself economically. One feels this power of the soil even more poignantly when one leaves the East and travels farther inland, toward the West.

As near the Atlantic as Chicago this attitude is distinctly felt. Formerly the East was economically and politically supreme, but for some time it has become more and more apparent that the Middle West is developing into a new and independent economic area with Chicago as its center. This area includes the states around the Great Lakes, as well as those farther south, in the Mississippi Valley. Chicago is now working towards a plan whereby the Great Lakes will be directly connected with the Atlantic by a deep waterway.

The Middle West is the most prosperous territory

in the United States, and promises to have an even greater future than the East. This belief in the future is stimulated in the Middle West more than in the East, for Middle Westerners, generally, feel that despite their present achievements, only a beginning has been made. Industry in the Middle West is still expanding rapidly, while in the East the competitive supremacy of a number of trades (the textile industry, for example) is now somewhat shaken by the opening up of water power in other parts of the country. In the Middle West the banks, too, are slowly but surely beginning to emancipate themselves from the predominating control of the huge Eastern banking houses. Bankers in the Middle West attribute this development to the fertility of the soil in the Middle West, where the wide productive expanse of the Mississippi River and its tributaries, unbroken by any mountains, forms the basis of all the wealth produced in this district. The development of industry, finance and trade, and the rise in consumption are all due to the great wealth produced by the soil.

In the Far West, beyond the Rocky Mountains, the soil has been responsible even more markedly for the great wealth which has been produced. This enormous territory, which has been closer to becoming a vital part of the country since the Panama Canal was built, and is centered around San Francisco and Los Angeles, forms the third economic area of the United States. Not much else, apart from rivers and their harbors, exists in this district but the wealth produced by the land. In Wyoming and Montana experts survey the mountains in the spring in search of ore, just as they did in the old days when the gold-diggers came to this part of the country. Well-informed individuals claim that even many Americans, especially Easterners, do not know how much unexploited wealth can still be found in these states, where the economic development, as in California or Oregon or Washington, is primarily due to the soil. Water in these states produces the necessary electric power; the forests produce the necessary lumber. This whole development is due, above all, to agriculture, which is the basis for the district's wealth, just as it is the basis for the prosperity in other parts of the country.

A European, who considers only the trusts and the activities of Wall Street, who considers only the super-European uncolonial factors in America, does not, when he thinks of America, remember the relative youth of this colonial country. The tremendous industrial and urban development in America often makes a European forget that even now many states of the Union are really thinly populated farmers' republics, with only a few cities, and that it is the farmers who create the laws adopted by these states. The tendency of America's economic development is clearly indicated by far-reaching measures for the promotion of agriculture, which have been adopted during the decade since the war and as a result of the world-wide agrarian crisis. It is evident that this aid to agriculture is typical of the colonial needs and the colonial possibilities of the United States.

AGRICULTURE

THE education of the farmers is the most highly developed aid to agriculture. It was not easy to realize this educational system, for the rural population includes dozens of nationalities and every farmer operates his farm independently, energetically and boldly, as is the way of emigrants, who, on the other hand, are distrustful, unapproachable and reserved. It is true that they were not bound to traditions, like the peasants in Europe, but nevertheless they were used to the various farming methods customary in the countries from which they came. How was it possible, in view of the great desire for independence on the part of the farmers, and their general distrust of coöperative organization, for them to develop a uniform system of farming adapted to the peculiarities of the American soil and the American market? It is true that only in the second or third generation of immigrant farmers the basis for such efforts has been developed.

Agricultural colleges and experiment stations were organized at an early date by many states of the Union. The Federal Government assigned tracts of land to these states and the money derived from the sale of this land enabled them to found colleges and experiment stations, but for a long time these institutions did not influence practical farming very markedly. Occasionally (Ohio in 1895) groups of students made a joint effort to disseminate agricultural information among the farmers. Afterwards the colleges themselves sent lecturers into the rural districts. Then separate agricultural organizations were formed, but at first a far-reaching, centralized association did not exist. Such an organization was founded in 1914, when the Federal Government, the various states, agricultural colleges and coöperative farmers' organizations throughout the country jointly founded institutions, which were permanently to educate and advise the farmers and to disseminate agricultural information. County agents, who are agricultural experts, act as full-time intermediaries for this extension work. They travel all over their counties (counties are similar to our "Landkreise"), act as advisers and encourage the use of the best farming methods and types of production, as well as the best marketing methods. Farmers' wives are taught home economics; clubs for farmers' children are organized, in which the boys and girls take up some secondary branch of farm operation. The educational work carried on by these agents includes demonstrations, lectures, moving picture shows, extension courses and the distribution of market reports and data.

Agricultural colleges are the intellectual centers of this far-reaching system, while the county agents act as intermediaries. In this way agricultural colleges have been brought into direct contact with practical agriculture. "The campus of Ohio State University is the whole State of Ohio," is proudly announced in a pamphlet published by the University. This attitude prevails throughout the Union. The first county agent in the United States was appointed in Ohio in 1912; in 1921 eighty of them were at work in this state alone. By 1923 there were 2,100 county agents in the United States and about 4,670 individuals who were employed either by the Federal

Department of Agriculture or by the state agricultural colleges, in connection with this work. Expenditures for agricultural education are still increasing. At first $10,000 was appropriated by the Federal Government to each state wishing to participate in this movement. Recently these appropriations have been increased to $40,000; $50,000 and $60,000 for the coming years. In addition, the Federal Government is now contributing an amount equal to the sum allotted by each state or county for agricultural education.

In 1922, when this work was still relatively new, the total sum expended by the Federal Government for agricultural education amounted to 7 million dollars. Including the sums allotted to their universities, the various states in the Union spent 9.70 million dollars during the same year.

In 1922, six hundred thousand farm children were organized in boys' and girls' clubs and the crops raised by these children were actually valued at 8.65 million dollars. As a whole, the practical results of agricultural education have been tremendous. Manhattan University, an agricultural college in Kansas, cultivated a new kind of oats, which yielded a third again as much as the oats previously planted in the state. In the course of six years 45 per cent of the state acreage had been planted to this new kind of oats. Agricultural education first taught individual farmers to plant this new variety, for they realized that it was more promising than the old; their success soon caused others to try it and thus the whole state became more productive. This is only one example among many.

Aside from this public organization helping the farmers to help themselves, funds and support towards an increase of agricultural prosperity are contributed by private organizations as well; and this is symptomatic of American economic methods in general. Railroad companies, for instance, realize that when the productivity of agriculture increases the volume of freight, profits will also rise. An improvement of agriculture, furthermore, causes the land owned by these companies to rise in value. Producers of agricultural implements and machinery realize that agricultural education, increasing the farmer's knowledge and efficiency, will increase his purchasing power as well, and that a greater demand for their products will result. It is for this reason that these producers as well as the railroad companies contribute to agricultural education.

The railroad companies employ publicity agents who advertise better farming in specific areas near the railroad. They also operate model farms to demonstrate the results of efficient farming. The agricultural machinery producers do similar publicity work. The International Harvester Company, the largest of these companies, has even organized an extension department which is administered by trained experts. The International Harvester Company does not advertise its own machines only, for in the long run the company will profit by the large sums spent on agricultural education in general, and for this reason the company works towards an improvement of agricultural conditions in general, distributes popular pamphlets on all kinds of farming subjects, arranges lectures, displays, statistical exhibits, and operates model farms. All these efforts illustrate what great possibilities (and what possibilities for greatness) are available for private enterprises, as well, when extensive capital power is con-

trolled by one unified management, which makes
plans far ahead.

In America all interests concerned coöperate towards the development of agricultural education: the
Government, the farmers' organizations, private
capital and agricultural colleges. The latter are the
most important factor in this work. Manhattan College is planning a two weeks' demonstration excur-
sion trip during the summer vacation. The instructors included in this trip are to travel all over
the state in a special train; they will make forty-two
stops, and if the weather is favorable it is hoped
that a hundred thousand individuals will attend the
lectures to be given in various parts of the state.
Trips of this kind are not uncommon in America.
During the regular vacations in the summer, special
courses are given for farmers at a number of agricultural colleges. These short courses, which are
free, are one, two or four weeks long, depending
upon their subject. Practical farmers, including
both men and women, attending these courses, live in
the college dormitories, otherwise deserted during
the vacation. The entire campus, in fact, is at their
disposal, which indicates to what an extent these
colleges really consider themselves as belonging to
the farmers, and to what an extent they are ready to
give help and advice in all practical questions.

All forms of agricultural education aim to make
farming more productive. All Americans, including
the urban population, are glad to coöperate in this
effort, for even the city dwellers realize that they
themselves will benefit indirectly from improved
agricultural conditions. Productive farming means
not only a high productivity of agriculture, it means
also that the commodities produced shall be market-

able and that they shall be efficiently marketed. The slogan of efficient farming is not "more bushels," but always "more dollars." For it should never be forgotten that farm products must be acceptable to the distant market which must first be won by a special effort. Nowhere in the United States is this principle more clearly felt than in California, where the fruits and vegetables, produced in abundance, would find no important market in this thinly populated state itself. These products must be shipped 3,000 miles before they are sold; it takes ten days to ship them to Chicago and twelve to New York. To compete with other fruits and vegetables marketed in New York, California products must be shipped in refrigerator cars, thousands of which are now placed at the disposal of California packers by the railroad companies. It is equally important that these products be of a standard quality, of a uniform mass production and uniformly well packed. These factors are equally important for other producing districts. American farmers had to develop uniform mass production, and so standardization became the great slogan of American agriculture.

The grading of world products, such as cotton, wool or grain, according to quality has been practiced for a long time. The trade gave the practical impulse for the grading of other commodities. The importance of the trade in America's economic system is reflected in this fact. The trade introduced brands which it advertised at great expense so that the consuming public acquired the habit of demanding these specific brands, which assured the purchaser that he was getting a uniformly good quality of goods. One of the results of this system, for instance, is the fact that American farmers do not as a rule produce any butter. They would not be able to market it, because people are accustomed to specific brands of butter, produced by the large dairies. The farmers, therefore, sell their milk to these dairies. The packing houses in Chicago also have gained control of the meat market very largely because of their well-known brands. They were also the first companies to use refrigerator cars. The packing houses are operated on such a large scale that they are able to market all their by-products advantageously. Nevertheless their success is very largely due to their brands. The successful marketing of California fruits and vegetables could not be achieved in any other way, but in California it was the farmers' coöperative organizations which, in time, occupied the controlling position, a position which in the meat industry is maintained by the large packing houses. For, whether it is a coöperative society or a private wholesale trading organization—which also exists in California—the slogan is the same; the brand is the decisive factor when it comes to marketing goods. The purchaser must know and trust the brand, he must be sure of the quality he can expect if he orders a certain brand. Only thus can many products be properly marketed. Private or coöperative trade agencies, therefore, deal in a limited number of brands, the various qualities of which are invariably the same. Consequently, and this is decisive, the producers themselves must produce this limited number of grades, if they want to make any profits. The higher the grade, the more valuable the brand, and the greater are the profits. Thus the trade is educating the producers.

A large fruit trading company which is able to compete with the coöperative associations operates extensive fruit farms in various parts of the country. The main function of these farms is standardization so that the farmers can see for themselves what kinds and qualities of fruit are marketed most advantageously. These private trading companies, too, standardize the farmers' production.

Americans use the word "industry" whether they are talking about agriculture, manufacture, about cattle breeding, peach growing or steel production. The use of this word has a real significance as far as agriculture is concerned, for the American farmer, who must consider the demands of a distant market, who must specialize and standardize his products, is in fact an industrialist. There would be no place in the United States for the hobbies of a German fruit-grower, who takes pride in the variety of his products. There would also be no room for the negligence with which he lets his fruit be ruined by harmful pests.

A uniform system of exterminating harmful pests is considered just as important by the American farmer as uniform production and uniform packing. Standardization is so far-reaching that the largest coöperative association in southern California, which includes about 70 per cent of the local orange and lemon growers, does not even permit producers to harvest their fruits by themselves. The association sends its own farm hands to do this job, so as to be sure that the oranges and lemons will be picked when they are just right for shipment. This association, with an annual turnover of between fifty and sixty million dollars, now spends about a million dollars a year on advertising, so that the brands produced by its members will become well known and will find a regular market.

The market is always the controlling factor. The American farmer has turned this economic law into state legislation regulating his production. Texas, the first state to pass such legislation, was not very successful at first. California, much younger than Texas, but a state whose very youth sharpened the business wits of its population, found such legislation successful beyond all expectation, "to promote the development of California's fruit and vegetable industry, to protect the state's reputation in state and interstate markets and to prevent deception in fruit."

California farmers adopted the first Standardization Law in 1915. This law stipulates the minimum requirements for the packing, shipping and sale of all the fruit marketed. Any one who did not live up to the minimum standards prescribed by this law had only the chance to eat the fruit himself. At any rate the law makes it impossible for him to spoil the market for other California products, for "nothing is more demoralizing to market conditions and prices than the movement of large quantities of products which are poorly graded, in bad condition, or otherwise undesirable."

The practical execution of this law, made even more rigorous by subsequent legislation, is entrusted to state inspectors. When asked, these inspectors issue certificates concerning the quality of the fruit inspected. These certificates are recognized by the courts if, later, any question as to the quality of the goods should arise.

During the last decade other states, following California's example, have standardized various agricultural products by law. In 1922 the Federal Government passed a law providing for national inspectors, who can issue certificates similar to the ones customary in California.

During the war national standards and grades, uniform throughout the Union, were introduced for a number of products. Afterwards, when the special wartime powers granted the Government were rescinded it was a question how many of these national war regulations would remain in effect. It soon became apparent, however, that interstate commerce was no longer possible without them. What is the use of standards and grades in the various states if these grades are so widely different, that grade I in one state implies a quality no better than grade II in another and grade III in a third? And what is the use of advertising an increasing number of brands without having a uniform standard of grades by which their quality can be measured? In other words the demand for national standards has been awakened and they have been widely adopted during the last few years. It now seems apparent that the states particularly interested will in future adopt an increasing number of national standards for an increasing number of agricultural products. These national standards indicate in detail exactly the quality a product must have to be included in each of the various grades. These standards are revised annually according to the year's experiences. It is decisive that all grades are uniformly adopted for all states of the Union, because, owing to the climatic differences in such a large country, the crops themselves are never uniform in the various states. In one year the best grapes harvested in California, for instance, may be classified as grade II, whereas Florida, on the other hand, might produce large quantities which could be sold as grade I.

Thus a minimum standard of quality is assured throughout the country for every grade of every product included in the standardized list. Every state, and every coöperative or private trade organization makes none the less effort to surpass this minimum standard, so as to make their own product more valuable. The market value and, what is more important still from Germany's point of view, the competitive value in world markets of American agricultural products, has been increased enormously by this system.

The Federal certificate of quality was the means to this end and the Department of Agriculture does not exaggerate when it maintains that agricultural standardization has been revolutionary. Though not prescribed by law these certificates are being increasingly used; they are, in fact, becoming a commercial custom. This is easy to understand, for a certificate assures the purchaser of the quality of the goods bought and enables him to sell the goods before they reach him. He may even sell them and forward them to another destination without having examined them at all. Litigation between the shipper and the purchaser is now practically impossible. In the report of the California Department of Agriculture we find the following lines:

"Standardization greatly reduces waste and losses, by retaining culls and unmarketable stock in the producing section, saving transportation charges and equipment, as well as other expenses of marketing worthless products. It gains a reputation for the territory and industry, improves market conditions by meeting the requirements of receivers, and thereby stimulates consumption, extends the market areas, increases demand, and secures the best prices available. Fundamental improvements in production and handling methods eventually will be the greatest benefits from a sustained program of standardization. The production of larger crops of superior quality will be encouraged, and insect pests, plant diseases, and cultural, harvesting, handling, transportation, and storage conditions controlled, in order to satisfy consumer demand, and secure the premiums paid by the markets for the best products."

In this way the farmer is sure to get a fair price for his products and this stimulates him to his maximum productivity.

Organized credit is another aid to American agriculture. Through his local bank it is relatively easy for an American farmer to obtain the regular credit he needs; that is to say—it is easier than it is for a farmer in Germany. Banks in America have not been consolidated as they have in Germany during the last decades, where so many private banks have been converted into branches of a few large banking concerns. In America the establishment of branch banks is against the law except in a few states. This legislation goes so far as to differentiate between commercial and investment banks. If a large commercial bank in New York or Chicago wants to include in its business an investment department, this department must be legally organized as a special institution. The securities department is installed in the same building as the rest of the bank and is practically administered by the same executives. The connection between the two is so far-reaching that stockholders in the bank must be stockholders in the investment institute as well. The stocks of both institutions are deposited with one trustee, who issues

the certificates, representing the shares held in each
of the two institutions. It is possible to acquire only
such dual certificates. In such cases the differentia-
tion between commercial and security banks is only
nominal. The fact that in practice it has been possible to circumvent the law indicates that it is not impossible for large banking houses to become more
or less closely affiliated with various branch banks.

It is true that even to-day New York banks very
largely control America's financial business. The
New York houses exert a decisive influence on short
term loans and at least so far they entirely control
large loans. On the whole, however, due to legal
regulations, bankers throughout the country are able
to carry on their regular business quite independently.
The tremendous size of the United States makes a
consolidation of banking interests, as in Germany or
England, impossible geographically as well as because of the large amount of capital involved. Some
people believe that the banks throughout the country
are too independent; they claim that there are not
enough able administrators to manage the 30,000
banks, now functioning in the United States, and
that the numerous bank failures are a result of this
inadequate management. But the fact remains that
bank consolidations are impossible, and thus the
decapitalization of the districts away from the large
cities, this dangerous result of bank consolidation, is
prevented. The nation's savings and working capital
accumulated in country banks are not subjected to
the centralized control of a few centralized powerful banks. Money accumulated in country districts
remains there, where it is used for the benefit of the
district by the local banker. He decides how the
money shall be spent. If he is clever he can invest

the deposits in his bank in a way which will be advantageous to his own customers. A banker in a small town or in the country can use his own judgment in extending credits to the farmers in his district.

This is probably why coöperative farm loan and farmers' savings banks, the most prominent among agricultural coöperative societies in Germany, which accumulate the farmers' savings and return them in the form of loans to benefit agriculture as a whole, are practically unimportant in the United States. Another reason why these coöperative banks are not more influential in America is the fact that the principle of unlimited liability in a community, which is the basis of the coöperative organization in Germany, does not appeal to the American farmer's sense of business.

To supply the farmers with credits the Government, through legislative action, has helped them in three ways during the last decade. First of all the mortgage credits, which had heretofore been extended by private banks or individuals, were organized. Before the war there was no basis for mortgage banks in a country like America, where the people as a whole were not a bond-buying nation. Capitalists on a small scale bought securities for purposes of speculation and not as long term investments. This attitude was considerably changed during the war. War loans revolutionized the investment customs of the country. For the first time masses of people became familiar with bonds bearing a fixed rate of interest. The Federal act of 1916 providing for land banks, was based on this new attitude towards investments. According to this law the country is divided into twelve districts and a land bank is established in each. These banks extend primary mortgage credits (the problem of organizing secondary mortgage credits has not been solved even here) to individual farmers. At first each individual could not borrow more than $10,000. Later, in 1923, this sum was increased to $25,000. Farm loan associations act as intermediaries between the land banks and the individual farmers. These associations, including the farmers living in one neighborhood, make a preliminary investigation of each application for a loan before passing on the application. These associations, furthermore, see that the borrowers use the money for the purpose stated when the loan was secured, they collect payments due the association every year, and act as custodians of the funds generally. In 1923 about 5,000 of these associations had been organized.

The Federal land banks obtain the necessary funds for these credits chiefly by the sale of farm loan bonds secured through farm mortgages. The fact that these bonds are tax-free causes the mortgage credit itself to become less expensive. Bonds of every Federal land bank are secured by each of the eleven other banks. This means that these banks do not compete with each other and that the bonds issued by all of them are uniform. The Federal land banks are administered and supervised by a joint administrative body: the Federal Farm Loan Board.

It was thus made possible to negotiate bonds free of taxation carrying an interest of from 4.5 per cent to 5 per cent, and to turn over these bonds to the farmer at a maximum rate of 6 per cent. In practice the interest rate is sometimes lower than 6 per cent.

The success of the Federal land banks caused a number of joint stock land banks to be established. These extend rural mortgage credits, which function according to the Federal act of 1916 and which are supervised by the Federal Farm Loan Board.

By the end of 1924 the Federal land banks had loaned almost a billion dollars to 300,000 farmers, and the joint stock banks had loaned another 400 million dollars. In other words this system protected the American farmer against loan sharks.

A second measure facilitating the granting of credits to farmers stipulated that loans were to have a maturity of from six months to three years. Regular banks were accustomed to prompter settlements. For this reason the Lemoat Bill of 1923 provided the establishment of twelve intermediate credit banks as adjuncts to the existing Federal farm land banks. The proceeds of the bonds issued by these intermediate credit banks are used to rediscount the farmers' loans which the banks have received from private banks or farmers' coöperative societies.

Financial aid to the farmers during their harvests is the third measure for the promotion of agriculture. This measure may in future prove to be the most important of the three.

A money shortage right after the harvest frequently forces farmers to throw their crops onto the market quickly. Often this depresses prices to the farmers' detriment, while, on the other hand, later price increases do not benefit him at all and are of advantage only to the commercial interests concerned. Wholesale trade in America, and especially the grain trade, has been protected against this possibility for a long time by the system of grain elevators and warehouses generally. The goods are delivered at these elevators, where they are properly stored, until their owner decides to dispose of them. He, in turn, is given a warehouse-receipt, and the grain elevator or warehouse delivers the goods only in return for this receipt. The owner of the goods stored can, in the meantime, use this receipt as security in obtaining credits from his bank. This procedure makes it possible for him to retain his goods until he believes that the best time to sell has come. In practice this system, which seems to be so very sensible, has been carried out only sporadically and irregularly. Local banks complain that they are swamped with warehouse receipts and banks in large cities often refuse to rediscount them at all. It is alleged in rural districts that the large city banks refuse warehouse receipts simply because they are so closely associated with the large mills and the wholesale trade generally, that they primarily consider the interests of these powerful groups. It is difficult to say whether this accusation is justified, and to what extent ignorance of the system or the banks' anxiety lest a sudden slump in prices might cause these receipts to decrease in value causes their refusal, but at any rate it is true that malpractices in the warehouse system itself have aroused a certain amount of distrust, and have discredited it among many people. The United States Warehouse Act of 1916 aims to improve conditions, by providing for "federally licensed" warehouses. The standing of the warehouse manager is investigated and the warehouse is regularly inspected. Definite rules and regulations must be observed. Uniform warehouse receipts are issued which must state the precise nature of the goods stored, including a description of them in relation to the adopted standards.

The meaning of the warehouse system in connection with the rapid progress in the standardization of agricultural products now becomes clear. The United States Warehouse Act aims in the first place to assure the reliability of the warehouses and their receipts. At the same time it aims to standardize warehouse receipts into uniformly negotiable documents, which can be transferred by endorsement, because they represent goods of a commercially well-known, standardized quality. If these efforts are successful the problem of financing the harvests will be solved, and the farmer will indeed be able to retain his crops for a considerable period of time after they have been harvested. This stage has already been reached in the case of cotton. Formerly cotton crops were financed by foreign countries to which they were exported soon after the harvest. It is symptomatic of the general financial readjustment, which has occurred since the war, that cotton crops are now kept in the United States, where they are stored, financed and later sold.

Warehousing is now becoming general for other commodities as well. This development is indicated by the fact that an increasing number of warehouse and grain elevators are voluntarily placing themselves under the control provided by the Warehouse Act. At first warehousing was usual only for cotton, grain, wool and tobacco, but recently an effort has been made to store other agricultural products, such as beans, eggs, apples, potatoes, etc., in a similar manner. An Act of Congress in 1923 furnished the legal basis for the warehousing of these commodities—and this legislation indicates another successful attempt at standardization.

Simultaneous with these helpful agencies the co-operative movement among farmers has progressed rapidly during the last decade. Towards the end of 1923 there were about 12,000 farmers' coöperative societies in the United States with about a million and a half members, and with a turnover approximating two billion dollars a year. The numerical increase of these organizations is not the most important factor, for during agricultural depressions the formation of such associations is only natural. On the one hand there are collective associations purchasing commodities of prime necessity to agricultural production (fodder, seed, fertilizers, material for packing, etc.). The first coöperative consumers' associations to be organized in the United States were among the fluctuating urban population, which had no impulse to save. For small purchases, consumers' associations, like the ones we have in Europe, are still practically unknown.

On the other hand there are sales organizations in the United States which market agricultural products: grain, milk, cattle or fruit, as well as coöperative dairies, cheese producers' associations and other organizations of this kind. Every agricultural product is marketed by a separate coöperative.

Members of these coöperative marketing societies usually pledge themselves by contract to sell their entire produce through the association. As a rule these products are pooled and then subdivided according to quality grades. (This, too, is symptomatic of the general effort at standardization in the United States.) The average price for each grade of the various products pooled is the basis for the payments received by individual members of the association, who are paid this average price for their share of the pool.

Usually the chief function of these coöperative marketing associations is to do away with the middleman, but they are also very important for farmers operating isolated farms, who without them might be dependent upon one specific purchaser. Coöperatives frequently install dairy and other equipment, and this common property is another bond uniting its members. But usually the coöperative's reputation and the reputation of the brand produced are the most important of its collective assets, for a brand must become known before the commodity can be successfully marketed.

All these factors are natural results of the system in general. A new development which did not begin until after 1920 is even more important. Two figures will indicate the significance of this new movement. In 1924 fifty recently established coöperative societies had a larger membership and a greater influence than all the other 5,424 coöperatives reported in 1915 put together.

These figures indicate that a new type of farmers' coöperative societies has recently developed in the United States: the gigantic coöperatives. Formerly there were only a number of small local coöperatives, which rarely coöperated among themselves. The new type of organization aims to market all the goods produced in one district or even in a whole state. These coöperatives are in fact huge, concentrated trade agencies of the farmers, which are administered like any business concern. The administrators of these agencies receive high salaries ($25,000 or more) and they must, of course, be very able executives. Considerable capital is invested so that the necessary warehouses, transportation facilities and other equipment can be purchased.

When these gigantic coöperative trade agencies were first organized their legal status was questioned. The anti-trust laws hung over them like a threatening cloud until the Capper-Volstead law passed on February 18th, 1922, regulated the coöperation of agricultural producers. The large California fruit trading coöperatives have already been mentioned. A coöperative association in southern California, which markets oranges and lemons, controls about three-quarters of the entire trade in this district. The California walnut growers' coöperative is even more powerful and now includes practically all walnut producers. There has been a similar development in other products. I am told that eight or ten tobacco growers' associations now market about half of all the tobacco produced in the United States. In the cotton and rice growing districts huge coöperatives are now developing. An even greater effort is being made to expand the coöperative agencies marketing grain.

Does all this mean the development of huge monopolies of agricultural producers? This question has been mentioned in Germany in connection with our own agricultural coöperatives, especially in connection with our "Milkring." In America the people concerned deny that this development means monopolization. Even if they occasionally allude to a certain similarity between these coöperative agencies and our industrial cartels, they emphasize that there is an outstanding difference between the two types of organization, for these American organizations cannot exercise any control over sales. They claim that with a membership of six million farmers, it would be impossible to form a monopoly, especially as any outsider can go into the business at any time. They maintain besides that anti-trust legislation makes this impossible. These people admit that it is permissible to advise farmers how to curtail production. Nowadays the Government is sparing no expense to keep the farmer informed, by telegram and wireless. He is constantly in touch with current market conditions, and it is believed that this should help to minimize the market fluctuations and to stabilize prices to a certain extent. But by constantly recommending the production of better and more saleable goods the coöperatives themselves are, they say, always working towards an increase in production.

Advocates of the large coöperative agencies like to tell one that once, after the war, when the grape growers' association in Fresno, which handled about 80 per cent of the total grape crop of California, wanted to maintain high prices for too long a time, the acreage planted to grapes was increased very rapidly. These grapes began to be harvested just as deflation set in, with the result that this grape district was temporarily ruined, and is said not even yet to have recovered. Many of the weaker grape growers lost everything during this slump. They could not even find purchasers for their land, and a number of banks, which had advanced them loans, failed at the same time. These bank failures, by the way, resulted in a movement towards consolidation of banking interests in California. The large banks opened branches, as they alone were able to curb the depression.

No matter to what gigantic proportions these cooperative sales agencies may grow in the future, at present the great struggle is the disparity between production and sales prices, especially for grain. American farmers, in common with farmers all over the world, resent the fact that since the war inadequate production prices have increased this disparity. In some cases this resentment has found a political expression; farmers and laborers have joined forces to combat the profits of the grain merchants and mills. This joint action resulted in the organization of the Farmer-Labor Party, which was unsuccessful in the last National election, but which none the less attained a certain influence in some of the northwestern states. The efforts of this party to improve conditions by establishing banks and mills controlled by the state governments were not successful. Other plans to stabilize and increase grain prices were discussed for a short time. One of these projects urged the Government to introduce a "grain dollar," *i.e.*, to guarantee a stable purchasing power to the price of grain. Another project urged the Government to organize a huge agency which was to purchase, store and export the surplus grain produced in America. It is not surprising that nothing came of this plan.

In the meantime the grain sales coöperative agencies are growing. One attempt in particular is significant of this movement. According to this plan a number of the largest grain elevators worth 26 million dollars and belonging to some of the most influential trade organizations, were to be turned over to a coöperative sales agency which was to be founded under the control of the farmers. The private business interests owning the elevators in question were to retire in favor of the farmers. This plan (a great many smaller grain elevators are already owned by the farmers' coöperatives) met with difficulties, because of personal differences concerning the form and the financing of the idea. This plan is none the less symptomatic of the present tendencies of farmers' coöperatives. The gigantic grain coöperative is progressing. First of all, an attempt is being made to establish coöperatives in the various states, but the problem of uniting all of them into national organizations is already being considered. It is a problem which will take years to solve, but what are years?

COMMERCE, INDUSTRY AND THE PURCHASER

THESE agricultural methods are symptomatic of the way in which America's economic affairs as a whole are conducted. At the same time agricultural conditions reflect the reasons for America's tremendous economic success. Economically this spacious country is a united area, one gigantic homogeneous market for American products. This sparsely populated area had to be organized into a market, isolated groups of people had to be won as purchasers of these products. They must continuously be educated in the art of purchasing and consuming the various commodities offered them on this market. Potential customers must be canvassed all the time, and this strenuous competitive effort never ceases. But if a producer or a merchant succeeds in winning new consumers for his brand, if he succeeds in making his name known, he has simultaneously created for himself the possibility of enormously increasing the production and distribution of his brand of goods. This, in turn, enables him to decrease his production costs as well as his sales prices, so that his reputation and the reputation of his brand gains an even more extensive control of the market. Thus his product may determine consumption as a whole; the taste and the habits of the entire country may, in fact, be influenced by it. Standardized and efficient organization of wholesale production or trade may thus result in a powerful influence towards decreasing costs in general.

One Sunday I spent many hours driving through the immigrants' districts in Chicago, where workers and middle-class foreigners, representing a few dozen nationalities, live separated according to their race, belief or color. Racial peculiarities were still very marked among the children playing in the streets, and more especially among the older people, who were enjoying their Sunday leisure and sunshine in front of their dwellings. Again these racial differentiations were more marked among the women than among the men; their features, the way their hair was fixed, the details of their dresses all reminded me of the countries from which they had come.

Early the next morning I stood before a large railway station in the center of the town; suburban trains, one after another, brought crowds of people to the city, where they fill private and general offices in the skyscrapers during the day. The procession hurrying out of this station was fantastic, thousands and thousands of male and female employees were hastening to the same kind of hurrying employment. Their walk from the station took a few minutes, then these thousands of individuals were at their places behind typewriters, somewhere in the fourteenth or twenty-third story of some huge building, and thousands of typewriters would begin their ceaseless rattling. Modern industrial organization, with its far-reaching division of labor, has made all this written work necessary; gigantic columns of figures and nothing but figures, have been set in motion.

The monstrous uniformity of these passing individuals seemed even more fantastic than their overwhelming number. It was impossible to de-

tect differences of origin in their faces, to guess
from which part of Europe they had come. Faces?
All the young men were shaved in the same way,
wore the same kind of collars, the same kind of hats,
the same kind of shoes, the same kind of glasses.
The appearance of the young women was even more
uniform. It is true that some of them were less
young and less pretty than others, but they were all
wearing this year's fashionable figure, their hair was
uniformly the color of the season, their cheeks and
lips were uniformly rouged, all their dresses were
cut on the same pattern, their coats were the same,
with the same narrow collar and trimmed with the
same fur twelve centimeters above the lower hem.
And young women all over the United States, from
New York to San Francisco, from the Atlantic to
the Pacific, in cities with a population of a million
and in Gopher Prairie, all have the same figure,
their hair is the same color, they have the same
rouge, the same dresses, the same coats, with the
same fur trimming. Heavens! How many coats
with fur trimming there must be in America!

The desire to be inconspicuous, not to be "different," encourages this standardization of the people's appearance. Among the employees whom I
watched in Chicago, as among employees everywhere,
the desire to remain inconspicuous is especially
strong, but in America, this wish is felt by every
one. The practical consideration involved, namely
that prices for articles produced in such large quantities are relatively low, is, of course, another factor
contributing to this development. Huge retail busi-
nesses, which have been so highly developed from
without for commercial reasons, were only possible
because of this tendency towards uniformity, but

they in turn caused standardization to become general.

The mail-order houses, centralized in a few large cities, are the most interesting type of organization distributing goods on a large scale. They have made it possible for people, especially those living in isolated districts, such as the farmers and the inhabitants of small country towns, to become consumers in the large uniform standardized market. From anywhere in the United States anything can be ordered from these mail-order houses: groceries and furnishings for whole apartments, automobile tires and pianos, clothing and jewelry, completely built garages, even large houses, which are shipped folded together, and need only to be set up at their destination, for every stake and every nail is in its proper place.

The main catalogue of the largest of these mail-order houses (Sears, Roebuck and Co. in Chicago), which is as large as the address book of a city with a million inhabitants, is sent out to ten million addresses twice a year. Including the supplementary and specialized catalogues, fifty million catalogues are sent out by this one firm every year. Customers select their purchases on the basis of these catalogues; usually they enclose their payment in the letter giving their order. Every order is attended to within twenty-four hours, at most, after it has been received. If it should happen that an article ordered is not in stock the mail-order house does not like to write and inquire what the customer wants; instead it prefers to send him for the same price the article in the quality superior to his order. A great effort is made to satisfy the customer's every wish:

"When our parcel reaches its destination in the country, it is like Christmas for our customers and were we to forget to send the cap for Bill or the apron for Mary the family's pleasure would be spoiled." If the customer does not like the goods after they have reached him he can send them all back if he wants to do so. The mail-order house not only returns his money but assumes the parcel post charges as well. This concern distributes more than eight million pairs of shoes a year; at certain seasons 38,000 pairs are sometimes shipped on one day. During one spring this concern distributed 800,000 yards of silk; 130,000 orders are filled on an average every day, which means 30 or 40 million orders a year. The standardizing influence which this concern exercises among purchasers all over the country can be imagined. Other mail-order houses exert a similar influence, and the local stores, operating in small towns, must of course always carry a line of goods representing the newest things from the cities, or they cannot compete with the mail-order houses. These large concerns set the pace which the small ones must follow. As a result the standardization of consumption made possible by the large mail-order houses is markedly increased, and consequently the education towards mass production is greatly stimulated.

Chain stores, which have recently developed very rapidly in the United States, exert a similar influence. These concerns, administered by a central organization, operate a large number of branch stores, all equipped in the same way, selling the same line of goods, of the same quality, the same appearance, and with the same packing. The largest of these concerns, the Great Atlantic and Pacific Tea

Company, is reported to have established more than a thousand new stores in a year and a half! Chain stores are especially common in the grocery business. (In Germany this type of chain store has also been introduced. According to a report made by Paul H. Nystrom, at the suggestion of the Chamber of Commerce of the United States, there are now seventy-five chain store concerns in the grocery trade, operating more than fifty thousand stores. It is estimated that they control about 10 per cent of the country's entire grocery business. His investigation estimates, furthermore, that altogether about two thousand chain store concerns are now in operation —more than one hundred thousand stores, all told.) Chain stores are especially common in the tobacco trade. It is reported that they sell about 6 per cent of all the commodities retailed in the United States.

Department stores which have developed in small towns and especially large cities have a similar influence on the standardization of consumption in America.

It is, however, a question whether trade or manufacture is the leading factor in this process of standardization, whether the trade demands standardized articles, or whether manufacture forces the distribution of its standardized products. As a matter of fact manufacture and trade are coöperating in this development. A number of the large mail-order houses and department stores have penetrated into industry; some of them have built their own factories, others own the controlling interest in certain manufacturing plants, which were careless enough to sell their entire output to some department store or mail-order house, with the result that they lost all direct contact with the purchasers. It is only the competitive spirit, forcing every concern to buy stocks as cheaply and as advantageously as possible, so that sales in turn can be equally advantageous, which keeps this whole system from resulting in monopolies.

Industry, on the other hand, has independently the idea of standardized production on a large scale; and extensive advertising has made the names and the brands of industrial concerns well known on the market. The method of creating a market is the same in both cases: incessant advertising, announcements, propaganda—until the brand, the name and the firm have made a suggestive impression on the minds of potential purchasers.

Advertising has become an independent science in America, which is taught not only at the universities. Large advertising companies maintain extensive departments to teach and advise their clients. All kinds of statistical material is shown the prospective advertiser; he is given an opportunity of learning about competitive conditions in specific localities, often distant, in which he wants to begin selling his goods. He is even told how to advertise so as first to stimulate local markets before an expensive advertising campaign is launched in the million circulation magazines. These large advertising companies sometimes send potential clients away at first, so that they will come back later regularly.

Posters, which are considered an important advertising medium, are often amusing for a traveler who reads them from the train window. "We have spent millions so that you can travel in comfort," a poster painted across the side of a house by a railroad company informs him. "Buy your trunk directly from the manufacturer and buy something to pack in

it with the money you save," or "Read it aloud:
Camel Cigarettes are the Best," "It is cheaper to send
your clothes to the laundry than your wife to the
hospital." In this way the customer is directly
apostrophized by all kinds of business enterprises
and in every possible strain, including a sentimental
invitation, extended by a real estate dealer in an
empty street: "Build your house here, you will be
happy." The masterpiece, in my opinion, was a sign
with which the owner of a wooden shack, selling hot
dogs, ice cream, lemonade, and other drinks, extolled
his wares. He promised "100 per cent Service" to
any one stopping in front of the shack. Nowhere
could one find a more pithy, emphatic combination
of these two words, which are more popular in
America to-day than any other slogan: *100 per cent,*
the great political slogan of post-war nationalism,
as in "100 per cent American," and *service,* the great
slogan of America's economic development "100
per cent Service!" It seems like a parody, like an
irony of life, that a poor sausage seller should have
invented this term.

For not only Ford recommends the principle (to
his customers) that "the only sound basis for any
business is its service to the public." Service dedicated to the public, for the good of the community:
this is the watchword, loudly and incessantly proclaimed everywhere in business, which penetrates
into American life as a whole. It has nothing to do
with the quiet selfless motto "I serve"; it is propaganda pure and simple. First of all this American
watchword serves as propaganda for propagandists
(Chambers of Commerce, clubs, public speakers)
who use it to appeal to the professional pride and the
professional honor of American business men. This

type of propaganda may be successful to a certain
extent, for it teaches them to live up to high business
ideals, it educates them to a high level of quality in
their production and their distribution. Then, in
turn, as everything in America is used for advertising, this slogan is used by business men as propaganda for the general public. A manufacturer, producing a new line of goods, bank directors or department store owners, who have installed some new
accommodation for the benefit of their customers,
every one and any one in fact who is trying to win
favor in the public eye extols his "service." It is the
constant aim in the American business contest to
offer one's own service as the best. The economic
basis of this constant endeavor is the great competition which penetrates all American business enterprise. Competition keeps Americans constantly on
the alert; they are always conscious that only the
man who really contributes something through his
business can compete in the market.

All this sounds somewhat paradoxical in view of
the tremendous trusts which have developed in important branches of American industry, particularly
as legislation passed in the course of decades to
combat these organizations has been relatively unsuccessful. For no one can doubt that this fight
against the trusts was ineffectual to a great extent.
Even if the Standard Oil Company was dissolved as
a result of this legislation and thirty companies were
organized to take the place of the original trust,
there is no doubt but that this was only a nominal
change, that the Rockefellers own and control these
"independent" companies just as they formerly
owned and controlled the trust.

The Sherman Anti-Trust Act of 1890 has been

considerably amended from time to time. Finally the Clayton Act, passed in 1914, which went into great detail, made "unfair competition" illegal. At the same time the Federal Trade Commission was organized to perform two main functions; in the first place it was to prosecute all business practices not in accordance with the Clayton Act, beginning with the simplest cases of unfair competition, including the settlement of the most serious cases where existing trusts were to be dissolved. In the second place the commission was to act as a standing committee of inquiry, which was to inform the President, Congress and the public concerning the general development and specific competitive conditions of specific branches of industry and trade. The commission must publish its findings in printed reports.

The Federal Trade Commission maintains a staff of distinguished experts and a large office force, and it has done extensive and valuable work in both fields of endeavor. The commission's investigations have already resulted in many voluminous reports; in 1923 and 1924 it settled 3,111 cases. Naturally, the commission's activities have met with serious opposition from big business. This opposition will not succeed in abolishing the commission because of the very active interest it enjoys among the farmers, the trade unions and the women's organizations. But nevertheless the commission must be prepared to meet other restraining influences, for it is not an independent organization, but a political body, whose members are appointed by the President. This means that if the party in power favors large business interests, the membership of the commission will not be inclined to be very active. Besides, the courts in America, which are easily influenced by the current political situation, are often inclined to favor the ideas of the large corporations. The country's general economic development is, of course, the decisive factor. If serious economic reasons make the concentration of considerable capital advisable, this cannot be stopped simply by legislation. It is a significant fact that during the last few years consolidation rather than competition has been the problem among American public utilities corporations (railroads, telephones). The prevailing political opinion in the United States is opposed to the nationalization of these utilities, so that even progressive states consider it their function to control the rates charged and to intensify the public supervision of these corporations rather than to prevent them from consolidating.

It is significant, furthermore, that foreign trade is no longer subject to the anti-trust legislation, and export combinations may be organized to form a solid front against foreign competition. These foreign trade trusts maintain central agencies, common representatives abroad, etc. The Federal Trade Commission of 1924-25 reports that fifty foreign trade trusts have been formed, including more than five hundred members, and with total exports valued at 153.5 million dollars (chiefly copper, cement, wood and foodstuffs).

At any rate it is true that there are powerful trusts in the United States despite anti-trust legislation; that is to say, there are a large number of gigantic enterprises in various branches of business which control a considerable proportion of production in their specific fields. The size and the influence of these enterprises as well as the large amount of capital at their command and the close connections they maintain with large banking houses cause these organizations to tend towards monopolization. Gentlemen's agreements regulating competition through friendly arrangements are doubtless not uncommon. The "Gary Dinners" attended by representatives of the few leading iron and steel manufacturing concerns, after which uniform iron prices were independently fixed by all of the groups concerned, probably still occur. It is probable also that such price-fixing dinners are not given only by the iron and steel industry.

Nevertheless controlling cartels, of the type which has developed in Germany, do not exist in America. Anti-trust legislation has been successful in this respect in the United States because it has always been backed by public opinion. Competitive freedom has prevailed despite the powerful position of big business, despite the fact that the growing demand for specific brands has favored their increasing distribution and despite the large sums which all large corporations are able to spend for advertising. Officially there are no large cartels in the United States, which, backed by a protective tariff, curtail production and fix prices. The size of the country and the manifold possibilities for production would work against this development in any case. A sharp, vital and strengthening atmosphere of competition, permeating American economic life, lets no one "go to sleep on the job"; it demands the maximum possible achievement from every one. In the sense that there is a tendency to improve consumption, rather than to control the consumer, the word "service," in America, service for the benefit of the consumer and the public generally, is not mere cant but a serious reality.

An American, whether he be a manufacturer or a merchant, knows that he must capture a market for his goods, he realizes that towards this end he depends upon the purchasing power of the rural and urban population as a whole. For this reason the American manufacturer, who, in specific cases, may ruthlessly combat higher earnings as far as his employees are concerned, does not complain about the generally high level of wages. On the contrary he praises high wages. The American merchant has developed a system whereby the purchasing power and the will to purchase are kept alive among the masses of the people. This system is called the installment plan of buying on credit.

This system is based on the psychology of the consumer, on his belief in the economic safety which he actually enjoys or thinks he enjoys. The American does not like to postpone buying the things he wants until he has saved the money to do so; he prefers to buy them with his income. If he cannot do so at once, he pays off his indebtedness in installments. Thus installment stores and the installment plan generally were developed. A purchaser can buy everything on the basis of an initial payment and monthly installments. Land and houses are sold in this way on a large scale. I was told by a furniture dealer that about 50 per cent of all furniture bought in America is bought on the installment plan. In the automobile industry the percentage is probably even higher. Clothing and machinery and everything else is bought in this way. It is no disgrace to buy things on the installment plan, it is a publicly recognized business method.   The banks are used to extending the necessary credit to stores selling their goods on the installment plan.

Large department stores also do not sell their goods only against cash payments.   Every reliable customer can open an account, which need be settled only once a month.   I know of a department store in a medium-sized town which runs a hundred and forty thousand accounts totaling on an average 1.5 million dollars a month.   Special information bureaux, reporting on the various experiences of all the business men in the town with their customers, are of great assistance and the merchant's losses from outstanding accounts or installment payments are extremely small.

A number of people in America complain that as a result many individuals live beyond their incomes. It is true that during business depressions, when incomes as a whole decrease, many articles bought on the installment plan are sold second-hand because the purchasers cannot keep up their regular payments.   In normal times, however, this system stimulates sales and the business turnover generally, and above all it encourages uniform, specialized and standardized mass production, which is the basis and the strength of American industry.   Thus mass production is based on the great size of the country. The relatively small population of the country, and the fact that the supply of labor is small and expensive has stimulated American industry to the highest degree of technical efficiency.

THE CONVEYOR SYSTEM

In New York subway stations there is everything —except employees. The huge main stations are like cities under the earth; long subterranean streets leading in every direction ultimately conduct the passenger to the upper world. These streets are lined with shops of all kinds. Everything, the cheapest and the most expensive articles, can be bought underground. There are many restaurants, inexpensive and expensive amusement places of every description. New gigantic hotels (2,000 rooms with as many bathrooms) are directly connected with these subterranean passages; it is not necessary to cross the street before entering the lobby above. New York, towering dozens of stories above the earth, has been extended deep down into the hewn rock; there are two or three stories underground as well.

Subway passengers are guided by signs through this labyrinth: "Follow the black line"—like Ariadne's thread—and any one losing it may be lost for half an hour. Service? Employees? Money can be changed at every entrance, but that is all. There are no tickets, no subway employees in the station itself. And of course the trains have only one class of cars—in which smoking is prohibited. After dropping a nickel into a slot machine one enters through a revolving gate. This method provides sufficient supervision; it is cheap and quick and saves labor.

The same system is being introduced in an increasing number of restaurants. There are no waiters. The arriving guest almost bumps against a huge pile of plates, knives and forks. Arming himself with these implements, he follows an orderly procession along a large counter, on which hot and cold food, vegetables, cake, fruit and beverages are laid out. He chooses what he wants and places the food on his tray. At the end of the counter sits a young woman who adds up the bill at a glance and places it on the tray. The only road leading into the restaurant is past her desk. In the restaurant one can sit down and eat the meal which one has brought to the table oneself. Again there is only one road leading out of the establishment: past the cashier's desk where the bills are paid.

This simple method has already been introduced in a number of stores as well. At the entrance the purchaser is handed a basket in which he places the articles he wants to buy. At the exit he presents his basket, receives his bill, and the articles are packed. Human labor is expensive and so Americans try to save it as much as possible. They aim to replace it by organization or mechanical devices wherever this is feasible.

I saw the tremendous mechanism by which Niagara Falls has been harnessed. Now part of the water flows through gigantic generators and a large district is supplied with light and power. When these generators had been completed human labor practically ceased to function at the falls. "Half a million horse-power here obeys one man sitting at a desk," the text accompanying one of the pictures of the falls informed us. And it is a fact, as our guide said, that ten men operate this enormous plant.

It is really not man, but only water and machinery, which are at work.

Even in industry there are large factory workshops in which there are no workers, for the machines function by themselves. The large mills where human labor is only needed to pour the flour into the sacks are examples. I saw similar automatic production in a wallpaper factory, where an enormous machine was working at top speed while a number of workers stood by with practically nothing to do. The actual labor necessary for the production of this wallpaper is performed in another plant where machinery used in this factory is manufactured. In the wallpaper factory which I visited the worker's job consists in seeing that the machinery is running smoothly. "When I see that they are sitting about with nothing to do I am relieved, for I know that all is well," the manager told me. As he happened to be a German-Swiss, he added with a little doubting sigh: "This, too, is a habit which must be acquired—one must get used to idleness during the whole working day."

As a rule this is a complaint rarely heard in America, for, save in exceptional cases where work means enforced laziness, the strain and the speed of work in the United States are very exacting. The acknowledged principle of employers and workers, on the one hand, is to extract the maximum output from expensive labor and, on the other hand, to give a maximum effort in return for the high wages received. The more intensive an organization, the more machinery it can maintain and the greater is the amount of capital involved. The more intensive an organization, furthermore, the more it becomes necessary to decrease overhead costs by a maximum contribution from labor. Factories like Ford's or the large steel plants, where the machinery never stops, day or night, except on Sundays, and where three shifts of workers are employed from Monday morning until Saturday evening, can more easily risk investing much of their capital in new machinery. The more often and the more quickly a machine revolves the less the cost per revolution. This is true also where human labor, the other part of the productive apparatus, is concerned. Work is never interrupted during a shift. Tools and necessary materials must always be near at hand, where they can be picked up mechanically, so that the worker need not take his eyes off his job. The right tool must always be in the right place at the right time; it is simply out of the question in America for an industrial worker to leave the bench to go and look for his tools; "if twelve thousand workers each save ten steps a day this means that the strength and effort necessary to cover fifty miles have been saved." A worker never carries the article he has finished to another place in the plant. It is his only function to stick to his job; other work is performed by others, unless the machinery itself can handle it. This means division of labor, which has been developed to the highest possible extent by industrial organization in America. Competition among the employees themselves, as well as factory organization itself, made possible by this division of labor, stimulates the workers to their greatest speed. In Ford's plant, wages are paid on an hourly basis and, contrary to the practice in many branches of industry, piece work has not been introduced. I asked an engineer in the Ford plant how they managed without it. "Well," he answered with a significant smile, "we have found a system which is so stimulating to labor that we do not need piece work. We have introduced piece work paid on the hourly basis, as it were. You will understand what this is when you have gone through the plant." And I did understand it after I had seen the conveyor system at work.

In Germany the conveyor system has been known for a few years, chiefly through Ford. Many people believe that he invented this system or that at least it is peculiar to his plant. This is a mistake. For as a means of carrying material and parts from one work room to another it has been known to a limited extent for a long time. Even the more important function of the conveyor system, the regulation of labor, has been employed in Germany, in certain forms, for several decades, in wholesale bookbinding establishments and other places. In Germany, where the conveyor was used only in specific industries, it was never considered very important.

In America the conveyor system has been in general use for so long that people do not remember when it was first introduced. They can only say that it was developed to its present state of perfection when wage increases stimulated labor saving and standardization. Even the perfecting of the system was not a specialty of Mr. Ford's. The meat packing houses in Chicago are equally dependent upon the conveyor, not only in the slaughterhouses and meat production departments themselves, but also in the numerous auxiliary plants, such as the margarine, lard and box factories. A conveyor of the most perfect type, to cite another example, is the system on which the organization of a huge mail-order house like Sears, Roebuck and Company, consisting entirely of clerical and forwarding offices, is based. Equally efficient conveyor systems have been adopted in all kinds of industrial and commercial enterprises, except that here the system is not the basis of the whole business as it is in the case of Sears, Roebuck and the other concerns mentioned above.

The point is that the work is subdivided into as many specialized jobs as possible. These specialized jobs are performed by a row of workers who stand next to each other. The part being worked is passed from one worker to the next on a conveyor, so that each one can perform his particular function in the article's process of manufacture. The conveyor started as a simple means of carrying articles, but became a tyrant dominating the workers. When the conveyor is speeded up the workers are forced to follow its dictates and to hurry with their jobs accordingly. The conveyor's speed invariably determines the worker's speed. If, for instance, a conveyor carries a worker sixty parts an hour—or rather carries the parts past him, for it takes them away from him just as it brings them to him—this means that he has one minute in which to perform each job. He cannot work more slowly, or the parts would be piled up in front of him, and his neighbors, too, would be held up, for they are just as dependent upon the conveyor as he is. The conveyor is the master. If the management in a factory decides to increase its speed by ten per cent, hundreds, thousands, or tens of thousands of hands, employed in the plant, must work ten per cent faster. The workers are bound to the conveyor the way the galley slaves were bound to their vessel. This—if I may be permitted to say so—is the idea of the conveyor system.

It should nevertheless be emphatically stated that the conveyor system's influence on the individual worker and on the amount of his work varies in different plants. This is chiefly due to the conveyor's speed. In some plants, occasionally after serious struggles, the speed has been regulated by agreements between the employers' and the workers' representatives. In such cases the conveyor is fast enough, but not exhausting, and it again resembles a simple method of carrying parts from one place to another. When a plant's output is to be increased, and an employer wants to speed up the conveyor in factories where such agreements exist, he must place more workers at the conveyor so that the labor of each will not be increased by the increased speed.

In other plants the inhuman strain is somewhat relieved by two or three reserve workers at the end of the conveyor who remove and finish the parts left untouched because the speed was too great. When there are no reserve workers and the regular workers have not been able to keep pace with the conveyor, they or the foreman must stop it temporarily so that they can catch up with their work, but no one dares to do this too often; the pressure exerted by the conveyor is too unyielding.

In plants where no agreement fixes the conveyor's speed, the system exploits human labor unmercifully and sometimes the strain is almost unbearable. In such cases the amount of work possible in a certain time becomes a question of experience. Competition among unorganized employees makes it possible for the employer to exploit their competitive effort. It is said that some plants employ their own record breakers, earning twice the normal wage by establishing new time records. The result is that the other workers, who usually produce a much smaller quantity in the same period of time, are forced to accept a lower wage. The smaller their jobs the more helpless the workers are to do anything about it. An employee explained his dreary philosophy of life to me in the following apt simile: "It is like wheels," he said, "large wheels are allowed to revolve slowly, but the smaller a wheel is the more rapidly it is forced to turn."

American factories are not welfare organizations, as Ford expressed it, and his engineer was quite right when he maintained that under this system piece work was unnecessary. In some of the Ford shops and in other plants I witnessed terrible exploitation of human beings by the conveyor system. The worst cases I saw were, interestingly enough not in an industrial plant, but in the Sears, Roebuck offices, where the conveyor carries incoming orders to young girls, who sort, register, separate and copy them, so that each order can be conveyed to its proper department, and so that ultimately all articles ordered by one customer can be packed together. In one hour the conveyor commands the girls in some of these departments to handle 350 or 400 letters. Watching them, one wonders what would happen to one of them if a fly were to light on her nose.

In other cases, the conveyor's speed is more human. It is not the system itself but the manner in which it is administered that is the decisive factor. The same is true of the way in which labor itself is molded.

In the great slaughterhouse operated by Swift and Company in Chicago, which in 1924 slaughtered 17.5 million animals, and which netted 775 million dollars for its products (in 1918-20, before the price decrease this concern's annual earnings were as high as 1,110 and 1,200 million dollars respectively)— two workers can kill 750 pigs in one hour. Not twenty minutes after the animal has been slaughtered the meat has been properly quartered and is hung up in the ice-rooms. In Ford's large assembling plant the frames are placed on the conveyor. They emerge at the other end as completely finished cars and roll into the courtyard every three or four minutes, where dealers are waiting to take them into their salesrooms. This is the result of the division of labor made possible by the conveyor system.

In the two cases mentioned labor is not entirely meaningless, for no matter to what extent the worker is concentrated on the particular part which it is his job to finish, he is nevertheless handling firm, tangible materials, whether he is cutting the rind from a ham with an electric circular saw or fastening his particular screw to the wheel of an automobile. He sees the whole of which his job is a part. Above all, his task is part of a series of jobs performed by a group of workers, and despite the intensive division of labor he feels a solidarity with this group and he retains, to a certain extent at least, the consciousness of his craftsmanship.

In other cases work at a conveyor is entirely meaningless: when workers of both sexes sit close together in front of the conveyor on chairs which they must never leave, and their job consists in working at parts the use of which they never know, for they never see from where they came or for what they are used when they are finished. It should, however, not be overlooked that labor is often meaningless even in plants where the conveyor system has not been adopted. In a factory which I visited, there was one department for drilling little holes into small brass plates. This job is performed with great speed and exactness by machinery. The workers—they were women—only had to put the little plates on the revolving disk of the machine. Naturally they had to keep pace with its speed, and this meant that brass plates had to be placed on the disk twelve thousand times every single day for days on end. This type of machinery has been even more perfected; two holes are drilled into the brass plate simultaneously. While the disk revolves to adjust the next plate under the drill, an apparatus, functioning like two fingers, picks up the plate which has been drilled and places it in a receptacle. Human labor performs the most insignificant of functions: the worker only places the plate on the disk. Perhaps this, too, will one day be done by machines. At any rate already there are cartridge drills which need only be filled. One man can serve, fill and supervise as many as eight of these drills at the same time, but as human labor is increasingly replaced by machines, this means that more machines must be built. This development, too, means putting on plates and drilling holes, and it results in a meaningless division of labor as far as the worker is concerned; it means an increasing number of tyrannical conveyors. More machinery would mean that one meaningless job would be replaced by another which is no more satisfying. Perpetuum mobile—does this simply mean an unchanging cycle? It does almost, but not quite, for labor becomes more productive—that is the result.

THE PROCEEDS OF EFFICIENT
ORGANIZATION

To-day America is an important exporter of industrial products. In 1924-1925 her imports amounted to 3,824 million dollars as against exports valued at 4,778 million, only 1,060 million dollars of which were foodstuffs, partly in crude condition and partly prepared; 1,394 million dollars represented exports of industrial raw materials. Exports of semi-finished products, designed for further use in manufacturing, were valued at 646 million dollars and products ready for consumption at 1,679 million dollars.

This enormous increase in exports of semi-finished and finished industrial products cannot be explained simply by an assertion that America is extensively "dumping" her products on world markets, which implies that high American import duties are keeping foreign goods out of the country, and are causing American manufacturers to throw the surplus products, which they cannot sell at home, on world markets at "dumping" prices.

Such explanations for America's increasing exports are too simple; they are merely an excuse for the slackness with which many people abroad accept this rise as an unalterable fate, instead of studying their own mistakes and omissions in order to overcome them. The United States, like all countries with a high protective tariff, undoubtedly carries on "dumping" to a certain extent, but this is not a decisive factor in the increase of her exports. The fact that there are no cartels in America, which could exploit this dumping, and the fact that markets for most products are not controlled by monopolies, but by free competition, the degree of which varies in various industries, contradict this explanation for America's increasing exports.

American exports are based on wages which, as I have mentioned, are nominally about four or five times as high as German wages. As far as exports are concerned, the relatively smaller domestic purchasing power of these wages is beside the point; the fact that real wages in America are not as much above the German level as nominal wages does not enter into the problem at all. As far as competition in world markets is concerned nominal wages are the only consideration, but it is a question how America can compete in world markets, as she does, in view of these high nominal wages paid by her industry. In this connection Americans often mention the extensive use of machinery and the relatively small number of workers employed by industry, which of course decreases the total labor costs of the goods exported. But this explanation is only half an answer. Labor costs are not proportionately as small as one might think. In 1923 the output of manufacturing industries (excluding mining, transportation and commerce) was valued at 60.5 billion dollars as compared with 43.5 billion in 1921 and 62 billion in 1919. These figures reflect the business and price fluctuations experienced in America during the period in question.

These 60.5 billion dollars produced by manufacturing industries in 1923 included an expenditure of 34.5 billions for raw materials, coal, etc. The value of the products themselves, therefore, amounted to about 26 billion, of which a little more than half was spent on wages; 2.80 billion dollars went to 1.27 million employees and 10.99 billion to 8.76 million workers. Together these wages and salaries amounted to 13.79 billion dollars, almost a fourth of the total value of the output of the manufacturing industries. Besides, a manufacturer using a great deal of machinery must indirectly contribute to the high wages of labor employed in the machinery industry itself.

These figures indicate that America's competitive ability in world markets (despite high wages) can be only partially explained by the extensive use of machinery and the relatively small number of workers employed by industry. The country's abundance of raw materials and agricultural products (which is somewhat counterbalanced by the huge distances and resultingly high freight rates) is also only a partial explanation for her strong competitive ability.

A number of factors have contributed to the development of America's real wealth: the size and the purchasing power of the inland market, resulting simultaneously in mass production and standardization, a highly developed division of labor made possible by a highly capitalistic organization of industry, and finally the ability of healthy, well-nourished workers to maintain a high level of productivity—all these factors coöperate with the country's natural wealth towards the creation of America's actual wealth. And what is the situation as far as America's surplus capital is concerned? All European countries are concentrating their attention on this part of America's wealth as though they were entranced; they seem to believe that capital from the United States can replace everything which Europe lost as a result of the war. They seem to think that this capital can cure the evils resulting from a disastrous administration of politics and economics in European countries since the war. Europe—let me repeat—is very much mistaken in this belief and it is high time for her to realize her error. America's surplus capital is now rather generally estimated at 10 billion dollars, though the country-wide optimism may have influenced this estimate somewhat. Unquestionably this is a huge amount; it is about equal to Germany's total untouched income before the war. But when this figure is reduced to its actual purchasing power, and when the fact that America's population is twice as large as Germany's is taken into consideration, it is clear that the per capita savings in the United States are not much greater than they were in Germany before the war, where, according to Helfferich, the national income increased annually by 8 or 10 billion marks. This would imply a relatively small increase in present-day America.

For the United States is still in the process of extending its sources of wealth. As I have indicated in preceding chapters, where I discussed various branches of industry, a great deal of capital is needed for America's economic development. Large amounts of capital are constantly necessary to house the population, to develop transportation of every kind, to increase the machinery equipment of agriculture and industry. It is not easy to supply this constant demand.

Before the war the development of this huge colonial country was financed very largely by Europe; America's railroads were built chiefly with European capital. To a more limited extent American industrial stocks were also owned by Europeans. All this is past. American stocks and bonds, formerly owned by Europeans, were used to pay for deliveries of war materials and for foodstuffs and raw material deliveries after the war. The mother continent can no longer finance the colonial country. On the contrary, since the war, America has become Europe's creditor on a large scale. America is now dependent upon her own resources for her future development. Her rapid economic progress during the last decade has made this independence possible. America is not, however, in a position to finance Europe to the extent to which many people seem to believe possible, nor is there any temptation for her to do so. For in the United States interest rates—the most significant indication of the demand for capital—are relatively high. Unless he invests in certain tax-free securities with lower interest rates an American capitalist can invest his money at home in first class mortgages at $5\frac{1}{2}$ or 6 per cent. In the West interest rates are still higher. A clever bank director in Chicago said to me, "It is much simpler for us to follow development in California than in Europe. It is not always easy for us to understand European politics and economics." Aside from more conservative investments there are plenty of opportunities to make greater profits from speculative investments of all kinds, so why should an American capitalist be particularly interested in Europe?

Far-sighted critics of the situation believe that in view of this great demand for capital at home American interest rates are more likely to increase than to decrease; they believe that the profits demanded on investments will probably rise as well.

Every one is agreed that Europe, including Germany, can import American capital only if European countries approach American investors in a business-like manner. Americans will consider European investments only if first class European concerns, with first class securities, can offer higher profits than they would get for their money at home and if European credit seekers live up to American business methods and rates of interest.

It should also be remembered that aside from Europe a number of other countries are competing for the American capital market. The United States' total loan issues in 1924 amounted to 6,327 million dollars, 5,570 million of which was additional capital and 757 million was refunding capital. 1,258 million dollars of this total (*i.e.,* 992 million additional capital and 266 million refunding capital) was exported to non-American countries. Europe succeeded in attracting only half of this total amount. 277 million was exported to Canada, 216 million to Central and South America, 188 million was invested in Japan and other countries. Only 578 million was invested in Europe. And during the first quarter of 1925, when total loan issues amounted to 1,243 million, only 144 million of which went to Europe, conditions were similar.

To a limited extent America's leading financiers are willing, temporarily, to tide Europe over her present situation. They are interested in strengthening the European market, which they would like to see more receptive. Even in 1924-25 more than half of America's exports (2,660 million dollars) went to Europe.

America is also prompted to help Europe financially during a transition period, because of a somewhat embarrassing situation at home, which is not yet fully realized: Though Europe's interest payments and payments for sinking funds are welcome, Americans are not at all inclined to accept imports of goods as payments for this indebtedness, which after all, in the long run, is the only sound basis of payment. On the contrary, instead of accepting a reduction of tariff rates, which many experts consider necessary to stimulate these imports from Europe, industrial and commercial interests in America are agitating for tariff increases whenever European competition is felt in the American market. The expenditures of Americans traveling in Europe, on the other hand, even if they are considerable, cannot balance this account in the long run. Therefore, America is inclined to postpone the ultimate solution of this embarrassing problem by temporarily exporting capital to Europe, but let me repeat: America is only willing to invest a limited amount of capital in Europe for a short period of time. "We Americans realize," a leading American financier said to me, "that one can't get rich by borrowing, but that, on the contrary, one can be impoverished by it." This was indeed the simple wisdom of the wealthy towards the poor, but it is none the less worth taking to heart. Europe, and particularly Germany, is not in the position which America, as a young colonial country, enjoyed when she was being financed by Europe. For America always had reason to feel assured that her increased production of foodstuffs and raw materials, made possible by this financial help, would enable her to produce negotiable means of payment with which she could settle her indebtedness. We must find a way of overcoming our capital poverty by our own achievements and our own ability to accumulate savings. In the long run America will neither be willing nor able to do this for us.

INDUSTRIAL RELATIONS

"THE labor of a human being is not a commodity or an article of commerce," the Clayton Act of 1914 announces solemnly, as though it were a new pronouncement of the Rights of Man. The market for labor (where in reality supply and demand continue to fix the price of this "commodity") could hardly have been appreciably improved by this beautiful phrase. But these words are only the introduction, the preamble to the dry sentences following, which declare that anti-trust legislation is not applicable to labor organizations. It took the trade unions twenty years to achieve this result, for until 1914 anti-trust legislation, unfair monopolies and unfair competition were interpreted by employers' lawyers, who were in some cases supported by the courts, to include the organization of labor.

The ardor of this fight, and the passionate spirit of the man who personified the authoritative part of the American labor movement for decades, are reflected in a brief summary of the situation made by Samuel Gompers after the victory had been won: "Men and women are not of the same nature as the things they make. Labor power is not a product— it is ability to produce. The products of labor may be bought and sold without affecting the freedom of the one who produces or who owns them—but the labor power of an individual can not be separated from his living body. Regulation of and conditions affecting relations under which labor power is used are a part of the lives and the bodies of men and

women. Laws which apply the same regulation to
workers, and to the products made by workers, are
based upon the principle that there is no difference
between men and things. That theory denies workers the consideration and the rights given to human
beings. It denies the freedom and protection of free
men and women."

The situation is similarly described in a report of
the American Federation of Labor: "The Sherman
anti-trust law was never intended to apply to organizations of human workers banded together for
mutual protection and betterment. That law was
intended to protect human beings from the power
and the rapacity of soulless corporations and trusts.
But courts by interpretation perverted that law, intended to apply to the products of labor—perverted
it to apply to the human labor power of the workers
themselves. By these perversions of the law the
courts placed in the same legal category the steel
worker and the steel rail he produces; the engineer
and the throttle he pulls; the carpenter and the saw
he uses; the printer and the type he sets. . . . Labor
is the great, creative, productive force of the uni-
verse. It is that which gives dignity, nobility, and
purpose to human life." The American labor movement as a whole is not particularly ardent; it is normally nothing more than a cool-headed business
proposition carried on like any other business activity in America. The sentences quoted above indicate, however, that in emergencies this movement is
capable of great heights.

Juridically American trade unions were recognized by the Clayton Act, but their *de facto* recognition, and their freedom to act as organizations, is
still refused them so extensively by American indus-

try, that as compared with the European movement, American trade unions are only beginning to develop. Iron and steel industrialists retain the most pronounced "lord and master" attitude; it is they who show the strongest resistance to the organization of labor. Steel producers refuse to negotiate with the unions and they employ no organized labor at all. In certain cases their resistance has gone even further: the steel trust has blocked steel deliveries to manufacturers who refuse to maintain the same industrial relations in their plants as those prevailing in the steel trust. This is an old tradition. Even to-day older members of the labor movement tell about the frightful Pittsburgh strike in the early nineties. Pinkerton, a professional agent, regularly supplying employers with strikebreakers and armed rowdies, who were equal to any atrocities, enabled the plants to maintain their own army and navy to fight the strikers. Real battles were fought during this strike; finally the workers were able to obtain several large barrels of petroleum, which they poured into the river and lighted, so that the whole stream was a mass of flames. The Pinkertons, who were forced to land were killed by the strikers, but then ten thousand militia men arrived and broke the strike, and this meant the end of the labor movement in the steel industry for decades. This was thirty years ago, but events of this kind are by no means entirely of the past. At the beginning of the World War, when America was still at peace and was making money, there was a large strike in one of the copper states. A minister of the gospel told me that here, too, the employers imported gunmen; two thousand armed men attacked the workers at night while they were asleep in their beds and drove them into a baseball field, where they were locked up. Early in the morning they were crowded into freight cars and deported out of the state—and no state authority helped them defend their rights. Even now, ten years later, strikes in the coal districts are not handled very differently. It is not unusual for people to be killed on both sides; no one is surprised by these violent deaths, not even the workers themselves, who know how to organize their own side if the employers make this necessary. This is the violence of colonials, who accept battle as the normal way to defend themselves.

In the summer of 1925, after more than one murder a day had been reported in Chicago for some time, the newspapers published an announcement from Illinois bankers promising a reward for the delivery of certain bank robbers, dead or alive. These rewards amounted to $1,000 for every robber delivered alive—but $2,500 for every one delivered dead. The bankers added in their statement that it was indeed a cold-blooded business to offer a prize for a man's life, but that in the courts the robbers would be given quite inadequate sentences. Besides, so the bankers claimed, the robbers themselves would have committed murder for less than $2,500. "We now make it as profitable for a policeman," the banks stated, "to kill a bandit as it is profitable for a bandit to kill a policeman." Is the cold hardness of the mighty gentlemen belonging to the steel trust surprising in a country where even bankers talk in this manner?

The iron magnates are not the only ones who are hard. In the Ford works, for instance, the following principle prevails: "Our workers are happy and have nothing to say in the factory." And throughout the country there are large groups of employers who still cling to their autocracy; they determine the working conditions and the worker can stay if he chooses or leave if he prefers. This attitude may result in a far-reaching exploitation of labor, or, on the other hand, in extensive welfare work, which is intended to compensate the worker for this loss of freedom by material advantages. There are all kinds of sanitary and hygienic advantages, charitable funds, cheap restaurants for the workers, stores in which goods are sold at cost, and in some large plants there are recreation and amusement departments as well. The employers hope that such welfare work will cause their workers to feel a solidarity with the plant, and that this will prevent unnecessary labor turnover. At least this welfare work is not discussed hypocritically. "The employees' health is good business," or "what we spend for the recreation of our employees we get back in the efficiency resulting from their contentment." . . . I heard statements of this kind while visiting numerous plants.

Side by side with this welfare work in numerous plants a system has been developed which is somewhat like our shops councils (but without their legal basis), called Shop Councils, Works Committees, Plant Assembly, or by some other name indicative of the "republican," "representative" character of the constitution of the committee. The function and organization of these works councils differ greatly in various plants. In some factories they merely function as a medium through which the workers can voice their wishes or their complaints to the employer: in such cases the works council is only a mouthpiece through which the workers can express

their dissatisfaction with the details of management.
Other councils have greater influence; in some cases
they include proportionally the same number of the
employees and the management's representatives,
and have the power to make decisions concerning
the complaints brought up in the meetings; in some
cases they also function as a committee of appeal in
cases of dismissals to which the employees object.
Some of these councils, furthermore, are empowered
to discuss actual labor conditions; such as increases
or decreases of hours of work, wages and salaries
in the light of current business conditions, about
which the members of the council are informed by
the management.   This advanced form of works
council has become increasingly frequent in American industry during the last few years; it has now
become an important new type of industrial relationship which has developed in the employers' fight
against the organization of labor.   It is generally
recognized that the purely autocratic management of
industry is no longer practical, and the employers
realize that they must negotiate with the workers as
a whole.   Nevertheless they refuse to recognize the
unions.   Employers want to have dealings with their
own employees.   The automobile king Bresnahan
declares in "Main Street," "We're perfectly willing
to talk to any committee the men may choose, but
we're not going to stand for some outside agitator
butting in and telling us how we're going to run
our plant!"   No outsider may interfere; only the
workers themselves, who are not influenced from
without, are eligible for membership on the works
councils.   Many of these workers' representatives
are more or less dependent on the plant, or at least
they feel dependent, because they are afraid of los-

ing their jobs; besides usually they lack the knowledge and the ability of a trade union secretary. The employer resists the professional, paid agitator, to the end. This attitude on the part of the employer is not the only factor retarding the growth of American trade unions. The workers themselves, as well as the tendency of the labor movement as a whole resulting from their attitude, have been a great handicap. To state the case schematically: some of the workers are too badly off to think of organization; others are too well off to see any advantage in organization, while the majority only consider their problems as questions of the moment, and this is the decisive factor.

There is one bitterly radical group of labor organizations: the I. W. W., the Industrial Workers of the World, which recruits its members chiefly among lumbermen, migratory workers and dock workers. They have been called homeless, wifeless, jobless; they have no roots in society anywhere, they are unstable, usually "hoboes," who cannot bear to stay in any one place for long and prefer to pack up their few belongings and move on again when hunger forces them to seek work. The I. W. W.s hate the established order, they proclaim the establishment of a new order out of the old. They want to abolish the wage system, they are syndicalistic, anarchistic and inclined to violence. During the war, when the Governments' power was increased in America as elsewhere, and this state of affairs created an atmosphere tending to repress all ideas which were not orthodox, a favorable opportunity resulted for persecuting the I. W. W. ruthlessly. After the war, as well, a number of states retained or passed laws making every expression of syndicalistic ideas illegal and punishable by law. All this mechanism was really not necessary to rob the I. W. W. of its importance. The organization was never large, and as a result of these persecutions and of the prosperity prevailing in the United States, the membership of the I. W. W. has decreased considerably. The organization itself reports a total membership of only 41,600 for 1920. Other estimates, which are probably exaggerated, fix it as high as 200,000. The I. W. W. never made much headway among the enormous masses of the lowest stratum of labor and to-day the organization is less influential than ever.

This lowest stratum chiefly includes immigrants and Negroes. These foreigners came from dozens of countries in as many phases of industrial-capitalisitic development; they are unskilled, they have no money, no knowledge of English, they are helpless and unaccustomed to American ways of life and work. They are the "scum," the lowest stratum of the American people. Their work consists in the hardest physical labor; in the coal and ore mines, for instance, and in the steel works or other plants, they perform the most poorly paid labor; in fact they are the humblest, the most extensively exploited type of workers. They are forced to accept whatever employment they can find. The strong among them regard this work as a transition stage only. They want to get out of the "scum," out of the depths. Their ultimate aims are not uniform. A land-hungry Italian in a large American city is content to work like a dog himself, so that he will finally have saved enough to buy a piece of land and become a farmer. He lets his wife and children labor as well, instead of thinking of their education. An immigrant Bulgarian or Roumanian, who digs copper in the mines of the Northwest for $150 a month, and who can easily save $1,000 or more every year from these wages, thinks of nothing but the time when he will have saved enough to go back to his old home and buy a little place with the money he has saved in America. The Greek or the Jew from Eastern Europe harbors only one ambition, and that is to save enough capital to open a little shop; while other immigrants look forward to starting some other little enterprise of their own. As a whole they do not learn to stick to one job; there are no legal dismissal periods in America, and an immigrant can change his job or his profession every day, if he chooses. One day he may wash dishes in a restaurant, while the next he may be cleaning automobiles; the week after he may be employed in some factory and a month later he may be a messenger boy during the day and sell papers or do some other job in the evening. As a rule these immigrants are not stable or reliable enough to form a basis for a far-sighted and concentrated labor organization.

It is a decisive fact that the attitude of the Americanized worker, who has left the "scum" far behind, and who is well nourished and well clothed; who has, in fact, become a "real" American, does not differ in principle from that of the immigrant, as far as the permanence of his occupation is concerned.

In America, where industrial and financial capitalism has been most highly developed, there is no socialist movement of any practical significance. Occasionally one finds small socialistic groups which keep their socialistic idealogy alive as a tradition. To a large extent these groups consist of descendants of Germans, who came to America after the failure of the '48 revolution, or during the persecutions under the "Anti-Socialist Law"; or they are formed by Russian Jews, or people of this type. Occasionally, but only rarely, one finds socialists among the intellectuals, but even among them a pale type of socialism prevails, a socialism which has become very mild and peaceful. A socialist movement with any depth of purpose does not exist in America. Even the type of thought, which is called socialism in the United States to-day has not been assimilated by the workers at all. Election figures indicate this fact, which was reiterated to me by every one, with a knowledge of the American labor movement, whom I met. They all agree as to the causes of this phenomenon. A labor leader concisely summarized the reasons why there is no socialism in America. He spoke to me pityingly as to a man from impoverished Europe, when he said: "Our workers are not permanent beggars"—as they are in Europe.

America is a colonial country, and her people are colonials, to whom European socialism is distasteful. An immigrant, who has severed all ties with his home country, and who, having come to his new home as a pioneer to build a house for himself and his family with his own hands, must by the very nature of things, be an individualist; all the more so, if he is one of the many immigrants from rural countries, where the peasants feel individually and not collectively. He is all the more of an individualist if he emigrated, just because his old country, as a state, tried to suppress his faith or his political beliefs or his personal liberty.

This point of view, passed on to succeeding generations, has a very great influence on the attitude of the American people as a whole. A common aversion to state interference often results in a solidarity among descendants of people whose background was quite different. The grandsons of British Puritans and English Quakers, the sons of German democrats or of Eastern Jews, who fled from the pogroms of Russia or Roumania, or descendants of Italians who left their country where there were so many large estates that not enough land was left for the small peasantry—all these people agree in their objection to state intervention.

Finally, the prevalent distrust of the state, as a promoter of social reforms, has frequently been strengthened by actual events experienced by American labor. Labor legislation is only beginning to develop in the United States, but if in certain states a law is passed supporting a demand from labor, it is always possible that the courts may counteract all the benefits of such legislation; there is always a danger that the Supreme Court, either in the state in question, or in Washington, may declare such legislation to be unconstitutional. I have already mentioned how unsuccessful child labor legislation has been on this account. The same thing has happened as far as laws concerning women in industry, the minimum wage and other legislation is concerned. If the Supreme Court decides that legislation violates the right of property or the freedom of contract, both vouchsafed by the Constitution, all political efforts to promote such legislation has been in vain. At every trade union congress, therefore, a protest is regularly made against this omnipotence of the Supreme Court, the veto of which is more powerful than that of the President. If the President vetoes a law passed by Congress, Congress can still pass it by a two-thirds majority. If the Supreme Court declares a law to be unconstitutional only one way is left to pass it, and that is to amend the Federal Constitution. This procedure usually seems so hopeless, that it is useless to try it, especially if the legislation concerned is some progressive law drafted by an individual state, where a great deal of effort and political education was necessary before it was passed in the first place.

Why, the trade unions ask, is there no right of veto as far as decisions of the Supreme Court are concerned, as there is for decisions of Congress or the President? The Supreme Court consists of nine members, appointed by the President, not always chosen because of their legal ability, but because of political or other reasons which he does not disclose to the public. Are these nine men, who often make their most important decisions in votes of five against four, more enlightened than the 531 members of the Senate and the House or than the President? So the American Federation of Labor is demanding that Supreme Court decisions shall be treated like the President's veto: if Congress confirms its decision by a two-thirds majority, then the decision shall stand. The far-reaching change in the Federal Constitution, which this would involve, is a long way off and American labor has, therefore, increasingly abandoned political methods and is turning more and more towards purely union tactics. Joseph Schlossberg, the executive secretary of the Amalgamated Clothing Workers, writes in an article characteristically reflecting this attitude: "The legislature may refuse to enact laws providing for an eight-hour day, factory sanitation, a minimum wage or prohibiting child labor. When such legislation is enacted the Supreme Court may declare it unconstitutional as it has done in one case after another. But the relief which is denied to the workers by the legislatures and the courts is given to them through the successful strikes or negotiations carried on by the trade union. In either case it is due to the union's power. The union thus does something which the state cannot and will not do—raise the living standard of the workers by reducing the exploitation of labor. As a result of experience, organized labor has discovered that trade union legislation is preferable to political legislation. . . . Industrial citizenship is more real than political citizenship."

This statement indicates that trade unions and the labor movement in America as a whole, except in isolated cases, are not considering state socialism. As far as this movement is based on fixed principles at all, it is based on the idea of trade union powers, an idea which can be carried far: a syndicalist idea, without violence, therefore is closer to the American labor movement than socialism; suggestions of guild socialism are sometimes apparent (and it is interesting to note that in regard to works councils, of which the employers approve because they dislike trade unions, this tendency towards guild socialism among the workers is not so different from the employers' attitude, and the ambition arises before American workers or their organizations to share the fate and the administration of the industry in which they are employed: thus to attain economic democracy in the widest sense of the word.

The overwhelming majority of American workers do not adhere to any fixed economic principle; their "leitmotif" is expressed in the sentence quoted above: we are not permanent beggars, we shall not be wage-earners without property for life; we do not want to stay where we are, and we ourselves, or at least our children, can progress, they may become merchants, manufacturers, physicians or lawyers or what not. This does not mean that American workers always assume that such professions must of necessity imply progress. In a colonial country the European disregard for hand work as compared with brain work, which is often a difference in name only, does not exist. On the contrary, in a colonial country material success is over-estimated. An average woman stenographer earns less than an efficient woman of the same age employed in industry, and a moderately well-paid white collar man in an office is not envied by a young industrial worker, who wears the same kind of collar after his day's work. The main point in America is this feeling of liberty and the freedom of choice. Without doubt this freedom has decreased somewhat since the free land in this colonial country was distributed, but the state of prosperity during the last decade has created a new kind of freedom to take its place. The fact that many are not able to attain this freedom does not detract from the decisive factor: faith in freedom—which to a large extent is based on actual freedom. This faith makes work in America less irksome; even specialized, soulless labor at machines is made easier; for no matter how depressing and degrading it may be, there is breathing space for far-sighted workers; they are free to move about and their working conditions are not a symptom of narrowness, fear and hopelessness. This feeling of spaciousness removes much of the poison from social conditions in America. Pedestrians do not feel antagonistic towards the people in automobiles;

every one who does not as yet own a car, definitely believes that he will possess one in the future. In the same way the masses of workers and employees do not feel antagonistic towards their employer, towards the capitalist in general, for every one wants some day to be a capitalist himself. Instead of class antagonism the numerous prosperous, hopeful workers in America feel a frank, honest business relationship towards their employer. This relationship can at times mean heated struggles for every cent of wages, but these controversies remain businesslike, they are without the deeply rooted, centuries-old bitterness, always present in countries where class differences can never be bridged.

Workers who feel this way do not think of trade unions from the European point of view. A European worker, believing in his union, with almost a religious faith, pays his dues because he knows that this sacrifice will some day bear fruit: if he himself does not derive any benefit, he hopes that his children, who will be workers like himself, or his fellow workers may benefit.

The American worker, on the other hand, does not think of his children in connection with his union; he is frankly optimistic for their future, nor does he think of his fellow workers, with whom he may not be united by any common idea. He pays his dues if he hopes for a practical advantage from these payments. This attitude had to be taken into consideration by trade union leaders if they wanted to work towards a development of the labor movement.

All this explains the relatively small membership of American trade unions. In 1887 the number of organized workers, for the first time, reached a million. In 1914 2.75 million workers were organized. Then war prosperity stimulated the unions in America, as it did everywhere, and in 1920, 5.11 million workers, more than had ever belonged to trade unions, were organized.

The reaction followed and employers began very energetically to fight the unions. They began their "deflation of labor" policy and they met with little resistance from these workers who had been organized a relatively short time. The number of organized workers sank to 3.78 million in 1923. All of these figures include Canadian labor, which is organized in the American unions.

In a valuable investigation, Leo Wolman compares the number of organized workers with the total number of wage-earners in the United States. His investigation shows that in 1920, when there were 26.08 million wage-earners in the country, only 18.7 per cent were organized (against only 9.4 per cent in 1910). If agricultural labor is excluded only 20.8 per cent (in 1910 10.9 per cent) were organized. 1920, it should be remembered, was the banner year for the trade unions. Since then the number of wage earners has undoubtedly increased, but the number of workers organized has decreased by more than a fourth.

The membership of the largest American labor organization, the American Federation of Labor, reflects this development. During the last decade this organization has succeeded in assimilating an increasing number of separate unions, so that in 1923 more than 80 per cent of all organized workers belonged to the Federation as against only 60 per cent in 1897. Following are the Federation's membership figures:

```
1902 ...................... 1,024,399
1914 ...................... 2,020,671
1919 ...................... 3,260,068
1920 ...................... 4,078,740
1923 ...................... 2,926,468
1924 ...................... 2,865,979
```

It has often been said that the American Federation represents the aristocracy among American workers. To-day the leaders emphatically deny this exclusive tendency and they emphasize that any white worker who lives up to the rules of his trade may join their ranks. Recently they have been agitating for an expansion of the organization. In future, therefore, conditions may change, but heretofore the unions included have doubtless held down the Federation's membership. "Almost all," writes Wolman, "exclude persons not yet of a specified age; some have standards of skill which prospective members must meet; others impose high initiation fees or require attachment to the industry for a specified period of years; and still others impose restrictions on entry based on the color and sex of the applicants to membership."

In other words, the A. F. of L. is primarily an organization for wholly Americanized workers, who have gotten away beyond the "scum" stage. The politics and the general attitude of the A. F. of L. were molded according to the attitude and the aims of these Americanized workers. In a valuable article, published in the *Atlantic Monthly,* Benjamin Stolberg very subtly describes, "What manner of man was Samuel Gompers." He formulates the labor leaders' simple ten commandments, to which Gompers adhered from the beginning to the end of his career: "Organize by separate crafts; fight for more wages; for fewer hours; for better work-rules; strike when necessary; break no contracts; obey the oligarchy of the elder chiefs; commit no adultery with socialists, anarchists, syndicalists, communists; covet not the function of capital; and abstain from partisan politics."

These commandments indicate how exclusively immediate aims were pursued: every problem which is not an immediate issue is looked upon with distrust. For this reason, for instance, the A. F. of L. is not a member of the Amsterdam International, which is considered far too political and too imbued with principles. Politics and principles are looked upon with suspicion by the A. F. of L., which wants to fight for immediate results point by point, step by step—this is what the members want and the Federation fights only for narrow and highly specialized issues.

Thus, the unions have developed a workers' constitution, as it were, which, very characteristically, determines industrial relations in the United States. The country is too large for the unions to wait until labor in each separate industry is strong enough to force the entire industry to negotiate and conclude general wage agreements. Employers in one industry too are rarely organized into one country-wide organization. So each struggle is fought out locally, in separate industrial districts, in separate cities, in separate factories.

If the workers in a plant are sufficiently organized, they will negotiate and, if they must, fight. They aim to turn the establishment into a Union Shop, that is to say, to force the employer to make agreements with the union as such, to adopt a scale of wages, hours of work and working conditions which are in accordance with trade union rules, and to declare himself willing to employ only union members. The unions aim to turn more and more plants, one after another, as labor grows stronger in a particular branch of industry, into union shops.

In this way entire industries may be gradually organized, and union agreements recognized by the employer and by the union throughout the industry may be introduced. This plan has been successful in only a few industries. Normally every industry includes union and non-union shops, in which no organized workers are employed, the union is not recognized, and the management has absolute power to determine working conditions.

Aside from these union and non-union shops, these closed shops and open shops, there are so-called preferred shops. These preferred shops acknowledge union agreements, in principle they are closed shops, stipulating that the union must be notified whenever vacancies occur. The union has forty-eight hours to supply the number of organized workers needed, but if it is unable to do so the management has the right to employ unorganized workers.

Not only do union and non-union shops exist in the same industry, there are also employers who have a union and a non-union shop in the same city. This means that he has one plant with organized workers and wage agreements and another without any agreement, where the workers are not organized. Whether conditions are more favorable for workers in one or the other of these plants depends upon business conditions generally and upon the labor market in particular.

Doubtless in such cases, as elsewhere, the unions

play a decisive part in the rise of living standards among the workers. Union agreements fixing wages and working hours in American industry are gradually becoming the basis for labor conditions throughout industry. Working conditions are being increasingly determined by agreements instead of by legislation. Agreements are beginning to be used as a means to abolish American labor's most serious menace, which is uncertainty, and the feeling that a job is constantly threatened by quick and violent changes of business conditions. It is very generally believed that a number of employers formerly exploited these fluctuations systematically to repress the workers. When, after a period of great prosperity, production was forcefully curtailed and a part of the workers in a plant were dismissed without notice, the employer had the upper hand, and even when the workers were reinstated after the depression was over, he could force labor conditions of his own choice upon them. Now employers are increasingly realizing that this policy does not pay in the end. Overhead costs are too great and fluctuating labor turnover too expensive for the employer, especially turnover among skilled workers.

Such losses are especially heavy when, as is quite usual in America, the workers are trained in the plant itself. In highly efficient plants specially and very scientifically conducted departments are installed for the workers' training. Every new employee is submitted to periodical medical-psychological tests, which indicate for which type of skilled labor he is most suited. Large sums are spent on this investigation and training. I was told in one large electrical plant, for instance, that the per capita cost of this system is between $10 and $300, on the average, a per capita cost of $81 for each new worker.

It would imply poor business management if the money invested in the workers' training were lost by rapid labor turnover. The trade unions themselves, however, have exercised the strongest pressure on the employers to "stabilize the job." This stabilization has become labor's new watchword. Labor agreements now fix the minimum weekly hours of work (38 or 40 hours) which employers must guarantee, and for which the workers must be paid even if production is temporarily curtailed so that they do not actually work the full number of hours. The fact that the trade unions are beginning to include the maintenance of unemployment funds in their agreements is even more important. In some cases these funds are supported by both the workers and the employer, in other cases the employer already maintains this fund by himself. In such cases the unions make the employer realize that it will be more advantageous for him to spend the money, which he must spend in any case, for productive work than for unemployment; he realizes that it will be better for him to stabilize employment in his plant.

As a matter of fact American industry is now beginning to stabilize employment. In contrast to former slack periods many manufacturers now aim to keep their plants running in order to replenish and increase their stocks on hand. A more far-sighted policy directing the distribution of Government orders and of orders for the equipment of the large industries is now being increasingly encouraged. Besides, market conditions and fluctuations are being studied and watched more closely than

formerly and the credit policies of banks of issue
are being adjusted according to these investigations,
which are working towards all of these improvements.

The beneficial results of labor organization are
most apparent in the work of the Amalgamated
Clothing Workers of America. This organization,
which represents a new development in the American
labor movement, is independent of the A. F. of L.
and developed, in part, in a struggle with the Federation. The Amalgamated Clothing Workers' union
is more full of life, more stormy and more radical.
For its members were not "Americanized" workers
in the sense that the members of the A. F. of L. are
"Americanized." The Clothing Workers did not
harbor an innate feeling that they must demand
American standards of life; they were the "scum,"
they came from the lowest stratum of labor, the
stratum which was most heavily depressed and most
cruelly exploited. In New York, where the clothing
industry consists of several thousand middle-sized
and small factories, these workers were chiefly immigrant Russian Jews, and later immigrant Italians.
In Chicago, the second center, where the organization of the industry is quite the reverse, it consists
of four or five large concentrated firms with huge
plants. Here the workers include immigrants from
all thinkable countries: forty languages are spoken
in Chicago labor meetings and photographs of typical members of this group of working people look
like pages from an ethnological textbook dealing
with the peoples of Eastern Europe. Poles, Lithu-
anians, Hungarians, Jews, Armenians, Czechs, Italians, Ukrainians, Russians, Slovaks, Turks and
other nationalities are represented. In a history of

his organization Joseph Schlossberg describes the
struggle of these people, especially in the ghetto of
New York. He was one of these people himself;
he, too, knew what it was to work for miserable
wages sixteen or eighteen hours a day in an ill-
lighted cellar; he knew what it was to breathe the
wretched air as he sat in front of a sewing machine,
so that he is well able, in a few pages, to describe
the life of Russian Jewish clothing workers in a
New York ghetto. He describes the feeling of helpless misery and the great desire to lead a humanly
decent life. These conditions have been radically
improved in a few years' time by the Amalgamated
Clothing Workers. Formerly the sweating system,
which was exploiting them, represented America to
these workers. They had so little power to defend
their rights that if the contractor disappeared at the
end of the week with their wages this meant that
they had worked for nothing; the manufacturer for
whom they labored, did not know them, he knew
only the contractor for whose dishonesty he was not
responsible. The workers, on the other hand, were
strangers in a strange country without friends or
protector.

The American labor movement as a whole considered them as contemptible excrement, it was only
known that they undercut wages. No one took the
trouble to tell these immigrant workers how they
could secure higher wages. They themselves did
not know what to do, they had come from Tsarist
Russia, the country of suppression, where there was
no freedom of the press, no freedom of speech, no
freedom to hold meetings; the country where there
were no trade unions. Sporadically the people's de-
spair broke out in wild strikes, but if the workers

lost, their situation was even worse than it had been before; if they won, on the other hand, the seasonal character of their employment made it impossible for them to take advantage of their victory: they were not familiar with the rules of trade union battles.

The Russian Revolution of 1905 helped them, for a new type of immigrant began to come to America. These were men who had been educated in the European labor movement. Gradually the clothing workers learned the art of fighting, leaders were developed among their ranks and a large strike in Chicago, in 1911, resulted in their first important partial victory. After another serious struggle in New York, in 1913, their organization in the East as well became more stable, and a year later, in 1914, the Amalgamated Clothing Workers was formally organized and has held together through all subsequent battles. The victory was won. In 1913 the Clothing Workers had no organization at all; in 1915 there were 38,000 members; in 1918, 81,000, and in 1920, 177,000. In common with all American trade unions the Amalgamated Clothing Workers' membership decreased somewhat during the years that followed. Nevertheless, the organization in 1923 included 133,600 of the total 165,000 or 175,000—80 per cent—of the workers employed by the industry as a whole. This is a very high percentage for any American industry. The rise in living standards which the clothing workers in America have experienced corresponds with the strength of its membership.

In 1911 the 54-hour week was general throughout the industry and many workers were forced to work as many as 56 hours. Now the 44-hour week has been put through long before work hours have been shortened to the same extent in the majority of other industries. The development of wages indicates the success of the Amalgamated Clothing Workers even more clearly. According to official statistics the average weekly wage for full-time work amounted to $12.30 in 1911, in 1922 it amounted to $31.91, whereas in the spring of 1925 the average weekly wage for a male clothing worker amounted to $42.93, and for a female worker $32.87. The average weekly wage for all types of full-time workers, male and female, was $37.90. Even if the fact that during the off season, for about three months, the workers are not employed on full time, is taken into consideration, these figures indicate a marked increase in the wage level as a whole. And the material success was not alone.

In this industry, in which not the slightest beginning had been made in 1911, the most far-reaching workers' constitution in America had become effective in a decade: This constitution stipulates that union representatives shall carry on negotiations with the employers, it stipulates furthermore that agreements are to be very detailed, that an impartial arbitration board or arbitrator shall make and decide disputes and shall supervise the execution of the agreement generally. This constitution stipulates that unemployment funds shall be maintained, and shall be administered by impartial trustees.

The psychological change among the workers during this one decade has been the greatest development. "Then," writes Sidney Hillman, the president of the organization, "a 'worker,' a little feared, hardly understood and never respected, without power to defend his rights and responsibility for whatever rights he had acquired. A 'worker' without a voice in the management of industry, capable of guerilla warfare and helpless to make anything of an incidentally wrested victory. A 'worker' and nothing else. To-day—a citizen of industry, respected, self-possessed, responsible to himself and to the industry. A citizen of the industry with a clear view of possibilities and limitations and with a keen, alert mind and an organization to match, for whatever opportunity may arise to harness possibilities. . . . The self-confidence the members of our organization have won, the appreciation of their own strength and the consciousness of power that our union implanted in our one hundred and fifty thousand members is the tremendous contribution to the assets of this nation that no emphasis is likely to overstress."

The "Big Four" (including the Brotherhood of Locomotive Engineers, the Locomotive Firemen, the Railway Conductors, and the Railroad Trainmen), with a membership of 500,000, the other labor group which has developed outside the A. F. of L., is the complete antithesis of the Amalgamated Clothing Workers. The Locomotive Engineers and Firemen are the most important of these organizations. They are the oldest unions in the United States. Their organization began way back in the sixties, and their initial struggles are long since past.

The Brotherhood of Locomotive Engineers includes practically all engineers: 97 per cent are now members of the union. The Brotherhood's organization is so stable and so generally recognized and respected, that purely organizing and union activities are no longer as important as they are among new fighting labor organizations in America. For this reason coöperative and professional problems have gradually become more important. Professional honor became the Brotherhoods' ideal a long time ago. Honesty, justice, sobriety and morality are the four pillars of the Brotherhoods' organization. An engineer who drank was expelled—long before general prohibition came into effect. The Brotherhoods demand morality on the part of their members, they see to it that a high standard of morality is maintained; they demand that their members shall pay their debts and their taxes and that they do their duty by their wives and children. In other words, the Brotherhoods primarily want their members to be good citizens, and the organization wants to help actively towards this end.

During the last few decades they have established large insurance associations, including life insurances and old age and disability pensions, which provide for the families of members killed in accidents. Now they are enthusiastically building up an extensive coöperative system. Raiffeisen and Schulze-Delitzsch rather than Marx and Engles are their idols. The members of these Brotherhoods are the connecting link between labor and the middle class and they are conscious that this is so; 80 per cent of the children of locomotive engineers now go to college.

TRADE UNION CAPITALISM

THESE tendencies, which have developed in the American labor movement since the war, are creating what Benjamin Stolberg has called trade union capitalism. He has described this development in the following manner: "These New Unionists are accepting the basic economic structure of American industry and are trying to work within it. During the last few years they have gone into banking, insurance, and business to the extent of hundreds of millions of dollars. They are developing the technical training and the vocational placement of their rank and file. They are organizing for greater political power. But, most significantly, they are beginning to collaborate successfully with Capital, in the only way in which collaboration is possible, by assuming Labor's responsibility toward production. They guarantee efficient production in exchange for intelligent and humane management. Here and there, especially in the needle and railroad industries, they are establishing boards of mutual control and impartial arbitration. And they share contractually in the resulting benefits."

It is a very significant fact that the A. F. of L. coolly rejects this new trade union capitalism; the Federation is in fact almost antagonistic towards it. It is also significant that the chief supporters of the movement are the two trade union organizations outside the Federation; the youngest and the oldest labor organizations in the United States. One with a membership which has risen from the "scum," the other including men who are fully Americanized; the most heavily exploited and the most prosperous workers in America: clothing workers and railroad men.

These two organizations are also the chief promoters of the movement which is the most interesting in connection with trade union capitalism—the penetration of organized labor into banking. Trade union and labor banks have been founded, the first having been organized in 1920, and by 1924 there were 26. Most of these banks are still small. The movement is still in its beginning, but the railroad men especially are operating very systematically in this direction. They include the various forms of bank organization typical of American banking in general. Are the workers buying up capitalism by buying out the capitalists? The publicity work connected with these labor banks sometimes sounds as though they were. "If twenty million workers save a dollar a week, our entire civilization can be changed in five years through our control of credit," or "if you will use the power you hold in your hands, in ten years you can control the financial policy of the United States."

Actual conditions do not corroborate these high-sounding phrases. There are, of course, some labor banks which exercise a real influence in favor of the workers. The example which is always cited in this connection is the Norfolk dock strike in 1920, which occurred during the open shop campaign, when the employers refused to renew agreements concluded with the unions. So the trouble began and most of the dockyards stopped work. Some employers, on the other hand, renewed their agreements with the union, and continued top speed production. The largest of these dockyards had been obliged to contract a bank loan amounting to $40,000, which was called by the bank to force the yard in question to stop production and take a stand against labor with the other yards. At this point the Mount Vernon Trust and Savings Bank in Washington, the first labor bank, which had been founded shortly before, came to the rescue: if a capitalistic bank can force a plant to shut down by refusing credit—the workers argued—a trade union bank can grant credits and tide over the emergency. And that is what happened: the labor bank extended credit amounting to $40,000 to the dockyard, and this credit won the strike for the workers. Other less important cases of this kind have occurred from time to time. During wage disputes, when ordinary banks have refused credit to employers who were willing to grant the workers' demands, labor banks were able to help these employers. The workers' threats, on the other hand, to withdraw their deposits from banks refusing credits were another weapon against this policy of intimidation.

Labor banks are very generally able to refuse credits or securities of various kinds, which they are handling, to institutions or individuals supporting activities opposed to the interests of labor. On the other hand they are able to assist institutions or individuals who are helpful to labor. Labor banks can give financial assistance to coöperative associations. To a certain extent they can promote coöperation between industrial and agricultural labor in the form in which this coöperation is urged by the Farmer-Labor Party. In general, however, the activities of labor banks for the promotion of labor have been extremely limited. So far, at least, these banks are not carrying out any particular business policy; their first concern seems to be to prove their general business ability. The impetus to organize labor banks developed from the unions' desire to use their large funds, their insurance moneys, etc., more profitably than was possible when these funds were deposited in private banks. Besides there was a keen desire to promote coöperation among union members. Labor banks are coöperatively organized in so far as their shares are held partly by the unions themselves and partly by individual members of the union, and in so far as dividends are limited to from 7 to 10 per cent and possible surplus earnings are distributed among the depositors according to the size of their deposits. It is not the prime function of these banks to make profits and the interest rates they grant, therefore, are somewhat higher and the rates they demand are somewhat lower than ordinary bank rates.

Labor banks cater to the needs of their member-depositors by facilitating small savings deposits and by granting them loans, at moderate terms, which are usually endorsed by other members of the union. The Clothing Workers' Bank in Chicago has made an arrangement with the Soviet Government, whereby money amounting to large sums may be sent to Russia. This arrangement meets the demand of the members who want to send money to their poor relatives in Russia.

Above all, labor banks educate their members to save by offering them the opportunity to do so and by a propaganda of thrift. These banks are also trying to win other sections of the population as depositors, so as to avoid the danger of a too one-sided clientele. But it has not been easy because of this one-sidedness for labor banks to use their money according to established banking customs. This difficulty is indicated by the extensive security investments made by the labor banks. As a whole these banks are far from being socially revolutionary in their present development; on the contrary they are a socially conservative influence: they are savings banks for the laboring classes.

While labor banks are trying to help organized workers to help themselves financially, and to train them to be little capitalists, another and much more far-reaching American development has shown this same tendency since the beginning of the century, and especially during the last decade. Public utility corporations, such as telephone, gas, street-car, railroad companies, etc., as well as industrial and commercial enterprises of all kinds, have been trying to interest as many people as possible in their shares. These concerns in the first place offer their employees and their workers all kinds of inducements to buy stock in the company: shares are divided into small units, a partial payment system for the purchase of which has been introduced, and these are offered to workers and employees at reduced rates according to their earnings.

These efforts aim to bind the workers or the employees to the concern, to make them actively interested in its prosperity, to make them "coöperative workers," as it were, an idea which is now very popular in America. It is interesting to note in this connection that here, as in the case of the Shop Councils, the interests of the workers and the employers come together, though their motives may be entirely different. It is therefore not surprising that occasionally, though not always, a highly developed shop council plan and a highly developed system for selling shares to the employees exist side by side.

But shares are offered not only to the employees and the workers. Many concerns mentioned go much farther and offer shares to their customers. "It is *your* enterprise; we are running it for your benefit; come and buy shares," is repeated by public utility corporations, taxi companies, even the large Chicago slaughter houses. A large biscuit factory, for instance, making a special effort to persuade women to buy shares, now estimates that about half of its shareholders, the number of which is increasing all the time, are of the female sex.

The purpose of all these efforts is quite clear: the concerns want to bind the customers to their enterprise, and thus to create mutual instead of opposing interests, for a mutual interest in the concern can most effectively prevent undesirable price discussions and can counteract any unpleasant suggestions of government ownership. The fact that this wide distribution of shares implies a constant source of capital is only a secondary consideration, which, however, does play a certain rôle, especially as the European market has been too poor to absorb American shares to any extent since the war, and as tax regulation, exempting many large classes of securities at fixed rates of interest, has caused wealthy people in America to buy these securities rather than the shares offered for sale by the concerns mentioned.

The actual success of the extensive distribution of shares among small shareholders is extraordinary. According to an investigation made by H. T. Warshow, published in the "Quarterly Journal of Economics," only 9.5 per cent of the dividends declared

in 1917 were received by individuals with an income
between $1,000 and $5,000 dollars; 64.7 per cent
went to individuals with an income of more than
$20,000. By 1921 individuals of the lowest group
received as much as 22.7 per cent of the total dividends issued; individuals of the highest group, on
the other hand, in 1921 received only 46.8 per cent
of the total dividends paid. During the following
year, the last included in this investigation, which
was the "deflation of labor" year, there was a slight
reaction: the smallest income group received only
18.4 per cent of the total dividends, and the highest
income group 52.5 per cent. Nevertheless the change
as compared with 1917 is most remarkable.

This tendency is indicated also by the number of
shareholders, which Warshow estimates at 4,400,000
in 1900 and at 14,400,000 in 1920. It is clear that
shares are passing from the possession of the few
into the hands of many workers and employees.
Are the workers indeed buying up capitalism by buying out the capitalists? There are sanguine people
who claim that this is the case, and who are already
estimating how few years it will take before certain
concerns will be wholly controlled by the workers and
the employees. In general the more skeptical point
of view prevails, that the controlling power exercised by big capitalistic interests has been strengthened rather than weakened by this distribution of
shares, because now the controlling interests in these
concerns are not forced to spend as much of their
capital as formerly on their supervisory activities,
and because the large number of small shareholders
is less influential and less coördinated in its possible
opposition to the controlling interests than a small
number of large shareholders once was. Skeptical

people believe, furthermore, that these conditions will continue for the present. According to their opinion the workers and employees will never be able to acquire more than 49 per cent of the shares —the remaining 51 per cent, representing power, will be retained by the people who are now in control. It is clear that this skeptical point of view is probably correct. So far the small shareholders among the employees of a plant represent, like the labor banks in their present stage, a socially conservative rather than a socially revolutionary influence.

The status of the American labor constitution and the labor movement as a whole is indicated by the conservative character of these institutions; and the majority of American workers, as individuals, are conservative, knowing nothing and caring less about the real meaning of a labor movement.

IMMIGRATION RESTRICTIONS AND THE FUTURE OF LABOR

DURING periods of war and post-war prosperity, conditions are such that sociological differences are temporarily diminished and far-reaching labor conflicts seem undesirable and not worth while. If one asks what America's future sociological development will be, one encounters two distinct opinions, which, at first, seem to be sharply differentiated.

According to one view America will follow Europe's road, despite all of the factors which sociologically now separate the United States from Europe. Adherents of this view go even farther; they maintain that in 1914 America was already beginning to follow Europe's example. They believe that developments during the last decade are only an entr'acte in the inevitable tragedy which began about 1890, when America's destiny changed and the available free land had been given away. Since then, when it became impossible for the huge industrial labor reserves to "escape into freedom," sociological evolution can progress only in one direction and the only factor, still undetermined, is the speed with which this development will occur. Classes of society are not yet stabilized, but they will be in time. To-day an ascent from poverty to property is still possible, but this is more difficult than it was formerly, and is growing more difficult all the time. America, like every capitalistic industrial country, will develop a proletariat, which will be condemned to a permanent proletarian state of existence. And then, these people believe, social problems and conflicts will break forth sharply—just as they have in Europe.

This is one prognostication, the seriousness of which is recognized even by individuals who themselves expect a different development. They, however, consider another date as the decisive turning point in the destiny of their colonial country. They believe that this point was reached when the American nation decided to end its colonial period as such and to begin a new epoch in its history by restricting immigration by a law passed on May 26, 1924. They believe that this law, which is so extreme that it almost ends immigration altogether, will in future mold America's sociological development. It is their opinion that these immigration restrictions will completely change America's sociological aspect, and that conditions will develop which will be quite different from Europe. I believe that this prognostication will probably prove to be the more correct one in the immediate future, unless America's prosperity should be fundamentally shaken as a result of the economic crisis in Europe; and that the influence of immigration restriction on social conditions can scarcely be overestimated.

Immigration restriction resulted from several causes. Nationalism, bred by the war, played a certain rôle in this development. Besides, Americans were tired of the squabbles among European nations. It was realized, furthermore, that for some time immigration from northern Germanic European countries was decreasing in favor of immigration from Southern and Southeastern Europe, including an increasing number of less desirable foreigners who were difficult to assimilate, and who were culturally less developed than the aliens coming from the countries farther North. Aside from these considerations Americans were afraid that bolshevistic ideas might be brought in by these immigrants, and a blockade of the country's frontiers seemed the simplest method of keeping out such ideas. But all these popular notions found an active expression only after the trade unions and the workers in general took them up and exploited them.

American labor exploited the favorable political situation and insisted that protective immigration legislation, to keep out competitive labor, should be adopted side by side with protective tariff legislation preventing the importation of competitive commodities. For American labor considered the immigrants merely as competitors depressing wages and breaking strikes. If labor had had its way in 1924 Congress would have stopped immigration altogether for five years or more. In practice the legislation which was actually passed does not differ very much from labor's original intention. The fact remains: this colonial country is making a complete break with its historical development and the very basis of its existence. America no longer wants to be the "New World," a place of refuge for the depressed and exploited, and the aim and the longing and the hope of daring people in old Europe. The people who themselves came to America for these reasons and took possession of the country are now locking the gates. They say that the country now belongs to them, that their number is large enough and that they do not want more immigration. America shall no longer belong to humanity as a whole, but only to Americans. American workers want to be by themselves and alone with their employers; they object to the competition which the immigration of starving people from crowded Europe would imply.

So far the sociological effects of immigration restrictions are not fully apparent. They are just beginning to be felt. In 1923-24 American immigration still totaled 706,896 souls, but in 1924-25 their number had decreased to 294,313; in fact, considering emigration during the same period, net immigration amounted to only 201,586—and almost half of these immigrants (130,193) came from Canada and Mexico, the two countries from which immigration is not restricted.

The importance of the immigration restrictions of 1924 is reflected in these immigration figures for the last two years, and it is even more sharply indicated by immigration statistics for the decade preceding the war. Following are the number of immigrants who came to America during these ten years:

1905	1,026,499
1906	1,100,735
1907	1,285,349
1908	782,870
1909	751,786
1910	1,041,570
1911	878,587
1912	838,172
1913	1,197,892
1914	1,218,480

The Immigration Law of 1924, representing the last and the most severe measure of its kind adopted, restricts immigration to 2 per cent of the foreign-born inhabitants of each nationality who were in the United States in 1890. The maximum from all countries subjected to the quota is 164,667.

With the fiscal year beginning July 1, 1927, this

maximum is again reduced to 150,000 and this immigration is divided among the various nationalities according to the national origin indicated by the Census of 1910. A subtle method in the computation of this quota provides that the more favorable position of Germanic Northern immigration, as opposed to the Latin Slavic immigration, will be maintained, as was intended when 1890 was used as a base. Immigration from Canada will not continue at the present rate; on the contrary, Canada with its extensively unsettled land and its agricultural possibilities is the aim of many Americans. Mexico, therefore, remains the one important source of American immigration in the future.

The Immigration Law of 1924, may, therefore, have begun a new sociological period in America. Heretofore the function and the result of the increasing use of machinery had been to replace skilled by unskilled workers; the machine replaced skilled work, and human labor was needed only to serve the machine. This replacement is already growing more and more difficult, because the number of unskilled workers in America is not being sufficiently increased from without. It is further possible to save labor by using machinery, electrical energy or water power, and other labor-saving methods, but they will not counteract the present shortage of human labor unless America's economic progress and her productivity unexpectedly suffers severe reverses. This inadequate supply of labor will become more acute and, simultaneously, labor's strength in its fight for its share of national production will increase. The possibilities for organizing labor will increase at the same time; for it will no longer be recruited from a constant influx of workers who are difficult or impossible to organize. The power of the trade unions will increase and with it their chances for success in labor conflicts.

This is the sociological development which many well-informed people predict for the immediate future. And it is a significant fact that to-day, when as yet the effects of the Law of 1924 are hardly felt, employers are beginning to oppose immigration restriction: their opposition is the indirect confirmation of this prognostication. A change in the country's immigration policy is, however, not to be expected in the near future, at least not unless industrial employers should gain the support of the farmers.

Inland migration has been increased by immigration restrictions: migration from the country to the cities, from the South to the North, from the East to the West. This migration can only temporarily weaken the effect of immigration restrictions; it cannot counteract it in the long run.

As yet, the "scum" of the working population is large; it will take years to absorb these workers but this fact does not change the fundamental tendency of present developments: American labor is preparing for a new ascent in the immediate future. This ascent will be a peaceful one if the coöperation between employers and labor, which prevails even now that the productivity of labor is increased, is maintained. This ascent may be violent, if the brutal and forceful methods, used during former conflicts, should be continued in the future. Future sociological problems in the United States, however, will then be primarily determined by one factor: the development of the birthrate and of birth control. For birth control is increasing.

THE AMERICAN WORLD

Americanization

WHILE visiting in a large agricultural state in the Middle West, which, when it was founded a few decades ago, included many Germans among its early settlers, I asked about the various nationalities represented in the population. My host, a college professor, did not seem to understand my question at all. "Oh," he told me, "there are only a few foreigners here; a few Russians, a few Roumanians, but the rest are all Americans—native-born American citizens." Nothing could have been more indicative of the prevailing trend than this answer. Immigrants representing dozens of nationalities have thronged into this colonial country, this enormous melting pot, and America will produce from this amorphous mass one uniform product: the American.

Until the war it was believed with a proud unquestioning faith that this result had actually been attained. "Every American who can trace his ancestors a hundred years back is the product of three or four different European nationalities," a leading merchant told me. Naturally this should not be taken literally, but frequently I heard similar statements and in specific cases I was often able to prove a mixed ancestry of this kind. Nationalities intermingle in marriage. When the children marry this intermingling process continues. And year after year individuals who have "arrived," the children of immigrants, move from their parents' national ghettos to the undistinguished districts which are fully Americanized. Before the war the melting pot seemed like an unquestionable reality, but this assurance was shaken when the war began. It is true that the second or third generation proved to be really Americanized, but many of the original immigrants, whose love for their new country had not caused them to forget their old one, were confronted with a serious mental conflict. Heretofore the United States of America had really been a United States of Europe as well: people with the greatest initiative had congregated here from all parts of the old world; they had rubbed off each other's differences, they had put their common life to the test. But when the old continent was so violently shaken the new continent inevitably felt these reverberations poignantly: many of the people who had apparently emerged from the melting pot as thorough Americans suddenly became separated again into different nationalities with conflicting sentiments.

Emotions had to be tremendously roused and extensive nationalistic propaganda was necessary under these circumstances to bring the country to the point of entering the war. And the effects of this nationalistic propaganda are felt even to-day. I have already mentioned that this propaganda was one of the factors causing immigration restrictions: if, indeed, the melting pot had not been as successful as one had believed, the simplest thing to do was to prevent new elements from entering the pot, so that the aliens already there could be assimilated without disturbance.

This nationalistic propaganda is still reflected in "hundred per cent Americanism" and in innumerable nationalistic organizations for its advancement—the

Ku Klux Klan, fighting against Negroes, Catholics and Jews with terroristic and intimidating methods, the American Legion and countless orders, alliances and clubs, including citizens' committees and chambers of commerce. All of these organizations have the habit of speaking about America in superlatives only, as the richest, the largest, the most efficient and the most powerful country in the world. They fill the good citizens with so much naïve self-satisfaction, that finally all the Babbitts almost burst with enthusiasm for "the ideal type to which the entire world must tend if there's to be a decent, well-balanced, Christian, go-ahead future for this little old planet" . . . for the "standardized American Citizen: fellows with hair on their chests and smiles in their eyes and adding machines in their offices."

To a certain extent this incessant spirit of propaganda permeates almost all American institutions; among a very large proportion of the American people it is engendered to such an extent that it has become almost unconscious. Individuals who come in contact with the public in any way, either with foreigners or their own people, appear to be wound up by a spring which enables them to stretch themselves and to appear lively, active and optimistic—their posture, their facial expression and their words invariably express a uniform satisfaction with this excellent American world. Especially as many Americans still lack a profound innate feeling of home for this soil which was colonized only a few decades ago, they emphasize their national solidarity, their Federal unity, with all the more assurance, and all the more optimism whenever they address the public. For this reason the Stars and Stripes are ever present in public offices and as often as possible this symbol is paraded on the streets. In the schools the hoisting of the flag by the best pupils is almost more important and more ceremonial than their morning prayer. And at school celebrations, when the flag is raised before an audience, men and women, as well as children, salute it in a military fashion, click their heels together, raise the right hand to a cap (which they are not really wearing) and every one is quite seriously imbued with the feeling that he is honoring the one thing which the schools above all, including as they do children of all races and nationalities, must promote and encourage: America.

Language is the most powerful factor in the process of Americanization; it is more influential than any propaganda. Nowhere can this be observed more clearly than in social settlements established in the foreigners' districts of American cities. Unselfish men and women, with a strong feeling of social responsibility, come here to live and to help. They aim to give these aliens, whose isolation and loneliness in a strange world seem quite hopeless at first, the first feeling of home and a community life.

Jane Addams' Hull House in Chicago is the great example. This genuine woman full of incessant activity has worked all her life to help the helpless. In her own district, in her own settlement, she has been able to watch the national synthesis resulting from changing immigration; she has observed the assimilation of these foreigners into American society as a whole. She has witnessed the gradual decrease of immigration from the Germanic countries, and the increase of immigration from the Latin countries, from Southern and Eastern Europe and most recently from Mexico. She has always made it her duty to give these new arrivals whatever she considered most important for them: when she saw that the Italians were not interested in scientific instruction, but that they wanted music or dancing, she gave up lectures, which heretofore had been the most important item on their program and gave them dramatic and other artistic performances instead. When she found that the Czechs had talent for industrial art, she established a pottery. In the spring of 1925, though she was sixty-five years old, this remarkable woman traveled in Mexico to study the Mexicans' habits of life. She wanted to be familiar with Mexican immigrants when they came to her settlement. This shows how seriously she takes her work.

Other settlements in turn are making a special effort to civilize the immigrants and to adjust them to American forms of life. A German visitor, who knows how the shortage of funds constantly hampers the work in Siegmund Schultze's settlement in Northern Berlin, is filled with secret envy when he sees the apparently unlimited equipment of these settlements. In one of them, in Pittsburgh, for example, there is a cooking school and connected with it a dining-room where the girls learn how to set a table, to wait on table and—how to eat. There is also a model bedroom, with beds for grown-ups and children, where the immigrants can become familiar with these furnishings and their use. There are playrooms with toys for the little children and work rooms with tools for the older boys and girls, as well as a few sewing machines for the women. There is a large swimming pool, a gymnasium, a dance hall with a gramophone and a loud-speaker, a library and a number of large and small clubrooms for the various groups.

Other settlements are smaller and more modest; their spirit differs according to the attitude of their directors; in their general aims, however, they are uniform. The foreigners are given the language of their new home. Literally they are given English lessons—for this is the alien's primary need, if he is to earn his living. The settlements also give immigrants from various countries their first contact with each other. Finally they introduce them to American modes of life by organizing them into the usual American clubs, boys' and girls' clubs, mothers' clubs, men's clubs, in fact clubs of all kinds and varieties. For the poor foreigner belonging to the "scum," these settlements represent his first share of America, which he can make his own—and in these settlements he begins to be molded into an American. This process begins with the language.

The schools, too, give the immigrants' children the language as their most important acquisition. And even the Catholic Church must adjust itself to this requirement. It is well known how extensively the Catholic Church encouraged and stimulated Polish nationalism in the former East Prussian districts by keeping the Polish language alive. I was told that in America the Catholic Church must provide the Italians with English-speaking priests (to this end young Irishmen are sent to Rome for their education). If this were neglected the churches would be deserted, for the children of Italians must and want to learn English. Without the language they cannot get ahead. And it is through the language that they become Americans.

On the whole, the aliens who are most quickly Americanized do not become the best type of citizen, for the initial Americanization harms them as human beings. They adopt only superficial American characteristics: the standardized forms—which undermine their old traditions and ties without giving them any new ones sufficiently profound or strong. It may easily happen that immigrants' children, who learn the language quickly, look down upon their parents—as Americans they disdain these aliens— and this younger generation which has no ties or roots anywhere frequently develops into the types of Americans who know nothing beyond the most materialistic desire to make money and to have a good time. An Italian priest was asked how America seemed to change Italians who, as is so frequently the case, go to America for some years and then return to the old country. What does America give these Italians? "It develops and emphasizes their innate traits," the priest replied. "If they were good originally they return as angels; if they were bad, they return as devils." A wise statement indeed! But it is clear that a rapid process of Americanization—especially if it produces a "100 per cent Americanism," which like nationalism everywhere is so utterly brainless—more easily tends to undermine good qualities and to develop less desirable ones. This development is the fate natural to a colonial country. It explains many of the uninhibited characteristics of American life. And, on the other hand, it explains the ties and prohibitions—in this country of freedom—through which America is trying to overcome this lack of inhibitions.

THE COLORED PEOPLE

ONLY one group—the colored people—is consciously excluded from the process of Americanization. The colored race which constituted America's original population, the red-skinned Indians, do not enter into this problem, for they have been tamed, and live on their reservations, not very differently from the way in which the original flora and fauna are being kept alive in national parks.

To reach the Tuscarora Indians' reservation one travels by way of Niagara Falls, but I am not quite sure whether it is not maintained more for the benefit of taxi drivers than to help the Indians themselves! For there is nothing Indian-like in this reservation where somewhat dark-skinned, black-haired people, dressed like other Americans, are seen operating their farms, which resemble other American farms with farmhouses looking like other American houses—in fact, as the chauffeur points out, these Indians live in an entirely "civilized manner." He stops in front of one of the houses, the chief's home. But we waited awhile before he received us, for first he dressed up a little, donning his enormous head ornament with colored feathers and his brown suède jacket decorated with glass beads. These ornaments do not, however, quite hide his standardized American collar, with a standardized American necktie over a standardized American shirt. Thus the chief of the Tuscarora stands at the door of his house, furnished like a poor, cheap village store, except that nothing is sold there; he stands behind the counter and makes a speech: "Here, gentlemen, you are neither in the United States or in Canada, you are in the Indians' Country, where we have our own legislation, our own government and our own administration. Thirteen chiefs and thirteen tribes live here. When the oldest one dies the oldest woman decides upon his successor. For our system is matriarchal, the son belongs to his mother's tribe and not to his father's. Once we owned all this country, but we loved whisky, and for it and for other things, which the white men brought, we sold them our land. We might have been the wealthiest of men, but instead we are the poorest. All of Buffalo is really ours, but the white men took it from us. But now they can take nothing more, for sales are no longer legal unless the President (he means the Commissioner for Indian Affairs, who protects their interests) gives his consent. Some of us operate our own land, others have rented theirs to tenants. This is the agreement we concluded with the President after the Civil War."

For a while the chief continued to talk in this strain, even after another chauffeur had announced more visitors. And while he excused himself ("I should be glad to tell you everything, but you see I am so busy") he showed us a flag, evidently embroidered by white men, the meaning of which was not easily grasped. The embroidery outlined the American eagle defeating a dragon representing whisky. Besides he exhibited a medicine chain, said to be a thousand years old, and other rarities, and while I was wondering, not without concern, which of them I should be expected to buy, the chief confined himself to offering me two post cards for half a dollar; he was much less expensive than the chauffeur.

Is this an Indian chief? When asked what he is doing here he answered quietly and proudly, "I live." This phrase was Indian indeed, for it was so very un-American. I could not get rid of the bitter after-taste which these words left with me; they contrasted so sadly with everything else. Indians whom a trav-eler encounters on the great transcontinental railroad routes seem sad as well. They sell fancy weaving and simple pottery—frequently decorated with black or red marks on a white or gray background on which ever-recurrent swastikas are apparently the most popular designs. Sometimes these Indians per-form their religious dances before a gaping audience, or, standing on the station platforms, they try to sell the same kind of glass beads to white people which the whites once used to steal their land.

In more lonely, more isolated reservations they live more like their ancestors. Some of these reser-vations, especially those on which oil or other treas-ures of the soil have been found, are very wealthy. The Indian population is now estimated at 347,000; their personal and tribal wealth on the other hand is estimated at 727.75 million dollars. Legislation, restricting the sales of their land, now protects these Indians, who are unversed in business matters. Wealthy Indians occasionally intermarry with whites, for as descendants of free men, they are not despised like other colored people. But is it really true, as the Tuscarora chieftain claimed, that they live?

The redskins have been exterminated or silenced —to the yellow races America is now completely closed. California, the State which felt itself to be most seriously threatened by Japanese immigration, has added state legislation to the federal law, which prohibits immigration from Japan. According to this California law it is illegal for a Japanese to buy, lease, rent, or own an interest in land or a house. Any Japanese in America, therefore, who was not born in America of Japanese parents and is therefore an American citizen in the full sense of the word, can earn his livelihood only as a wage or salary earner. His wife cannot follow him to America. America is really closed against Japanese immigration.

In the East there is much talk that a war will inevitably result from these conditions: doubtless this possibility is not unwelcome to people interested in war industries and in the expansion of America's military power. In the West, where people are more closely in touch with what is actually happening, they are much less panicky: no one in this part of the country has any objection to trading with China or Japan. But the decision to keep out the Japanese is considered none the less irrevocable by all sections of the population. Labor is afraid of competition from these cheap, modest yellow workers. "Meat versus rice" is the motto of American labor as far as the Japanese are concerned and, above all, America is to remain the land of white men forever.

As a matter of fact, however, there is in America a black as well as a white population. According to official statistics there were 10.5 million Negroes in the United States in 1920, which means that every tenth American is colored. No problem hanging over the country is as threatening as the Negro problem. This problem indicates how a wrong, once committed by a people, can go on poisoning them from generation to generation. Slaves were imported into Southern States as plantation labor. The Northern victory in the Civil War, which was fought from 1860-65, abolished slavery, freed the slaves and made them citizens. But the juridical change of their status did not alter the feelings or customs towards them. The Constitution proclaimed them as equals, but in practice, the attitude of the whites continued to outlaw them. In practices they continued to be outlaws, humanly and socially they remained a lower class, and economically they were exploited as before. The Negroes have the right to vote, but where they are so numerous that they might endanger the white men's control, they are again and again forcibly terrorized and prevented from casting their ballots. The Negroes are free, but in the South they are not allowed to ride in street-cars or trains with the whites, they may not eat in restaurants frequented by whites, they cannot live in the quarters where white men live. The Negroes are citizens, but in the South they are methodically kept ignorant: these states spend many times as much for the education of white as for black children. The Negroes may work and actually white and colored labor work side by side in many factories. But the unions do not admit them as members.

The suppression of the colored people corrupts the thoughts and feelings of the whites. In a Quaker college in Pennsylvania, one of the most highly respected institutions of its kind in the country, colored students are not admitted, but, as is frequently the case, the white students are waited upon by young colored people of the same age. "Colored people are splendid waiters and we love them for it." Emotionally the prevalent attitude is just as it was at the time of "Uncle Tom's Cabin": at best theirs is a paternalistic attitude, in which the idea of a possible equality simply does not enter in at all. And the professor who made the statement, mentioned above, about the Negroes, was one of the most cultured and finest men I know—he was a real Quaker but he did not even realize the meaning of his words.

Before the war the Negro problem was chiefly confined to the South. In the North the number of colored people among the population was relatively small so that the problem was not important. But since the war conditions in the North have changed. During the war, industry in the Northeast brought up a great many Negroes from the South to compensate for the prevailing labor shortage. This migration has continued since. In the North, negroes are relatively more fairly treated and receive higher wages than they do in the South. Immigration restrictions encourage this migration of the Negroes to the North, for industry needs labor, and as long as the trade unions haughtily exclude colored workers from their ranks employers will be eager to increase the number of their cheap unorganized colored employees. The employers could not find better strike-breakers and wage-cutters than these people who are really furnished them by the unions.

The shortage of domestic help also encourages this migration: the number of colored people in domestic service is increasing in Northern cities. Usually these domestic servants do not live in the houses where they are employed; they work for a certain number of hours a day and return to the colored

district at night. Thus the Negro problem is beginning to poison the North as well as the South. And
the descendants of Lincoln's generation who freed
the Negroes with their own blood are now overbear-
ing in their contempt for the Negroes. They practice injustice, brutality and suppression. There are
isolated white people who protest against these conditions, who demand that the Negroes be treated
with humanity and justice. But so far these people
are only a small minority.

When I arrived in Detroit the following incident
had just occurred: a colored physician, a well-edu-
cated man, had bought a house in one of the better
sections of the town, where wealthy white people live
in valuable homes. The next morning five thousand
people congregated uproariously in this street; they
threw stones, breaking every window in his house;
and when he was getting into his car a stone hit him
in the face as well, so that he drove off bleeding.
People wanted to force him to give up his house.
Material interests were added to racial prejudice:
the whites owning houses were afraid that the value
of their property would decrease if a Negro moved
into their street and so they backed the mob.

The restriction of the Negroes to residence quarters of their own is another means used to exploit
them: if houses in new colored districts become
cheap this does not prevent the colored people from
being charged high rents, for the demand for Negro homes is much greater than the supply. In business of this kind, which white landlords seem particularly to favor, they seem to forget their race
prejudices altogether.

The suppression of the colored people is most
painful for Negroes who are well educated. In the

South their schools are separated, but in the North black and white children often go to the same schools. Many colleges and universities in the North admit colored students (they are only excluded from fraternities and other humanly sociable organizations). In other parts of the country there are special Negro colleges. But, when colored boys or girls have completed their training, it is terribly hard for them to find employment in which their education will count for something. Gradually some of the colored people too are becoming prosperous or even wealthy. This cannot be prevented, but it can be made difficult. And custom tries her best to make it hard. Even offices belonging to white men are usually closed to Negroes. The Negroes shall serve in the home, in sleeping or dining cars or in cheap restaurants. Employers are quite willing that Negroes shall perform the hardest physical labor, which the white American worker does not like to do. When the Negroes demand a better chance, the solidarity of white society rejects them with a scornful jeer. Again and again the Negro comes face to face with locked doors. Again and again he knocks his head until it is sore against invisible walls which seem to shout out at him, "Down, down with you." And if he does not obey this command, he encounters humiliations at every turn.

The congress of a pacifist women's organization (of course this was in the North and not in the South) was attended by two highly educated Negro delegates. Naturally they could not live with the others, but when they entered the hotel, where the congress was being held on the second floor, the white elevator boy refused to take them up—he told them that the elevator (elevator boys are very frequently colored) was only to be used for white guests. It is easy to imagine the bitterness which such incidents call forth among Negro intellectuals, whose number is still relatively small.

Many Southerners were opposed to teaching Negroes how to use arms during the war: in the South people knew best why they wanted to prevent this by all means. And some day the Negro problem may become a tragic danger for America, for the fact remains that there are millions of colored people in the country. They did not come of their own free will. There seems to be no tendency among them to emigrate to their old African home. But the farther they get away from slavery, the more poignantly they will feel their present oppression.

GERMAN-AMERICANS, ANGLO-AMERI-
CANS AND AMERICANS

WHEN a young man heard us speaking German he moved closer to us in the bus. We chatted for a while and finally he said: "Yes, my father came from Germany, he fought in the War of 1870-71. Now I have been in the war too—but I fought on the other side." And this is not the worst tragedy for German-Americans, for this young man's mother is an American; his father is dead, and he himself is simply an American, he speaks only English and knows nothing about Germany: he is only somewhat surprised at the strange ways of Fate.

The older generation of German-Americans, the fathers and mothers, experienced a very real tragic conflict during the last ten years. Their bitterness indicates how many citizens' moral support America lost during the war and because of her participation in it, for the German-Americans have always been an important and very valuable element in America's population.

In Germany, during the last few years, the situation of German-Americans in the United States has been frequently misjudged. The Germans at home simply considered that there were, after all, millions of Germans in America—people in Germany thought this was all there was to it. Actually, even before the war, the situation was very different.

There were two main periods of German emigration. One occurred in the middle of the last century, when economic pressure before the Revolution of 1848 and political-economic distress afterwards caused many Germans to cross the ocean. In 1854 emigration was as high as 250,000.

The second period occurred during the late sixties, when the average annual number of emigrants amounted to about 130,000. During the early seventies emigration temporarily decreased, but it rose again after 1880. In 1881, 220,000 individuals emigrated from Germany and even as late as 1891-92 they totaled about 120,000 each year. This was during Germany's period of industrial awakening. After industry had been gradually adjusted, the secret whereby Germany's growing population could be provided for at home was discovered when the country began to participate in world trade. Since then, until the war, there was no emigration from Germany worth mentioning.

Germany's emigration fluctuates between 20,000 and 30,000 a year. These emigrants, as a rule, left home because they had relatives abroad, or because some German concern had opened up a branch, or because of similar reasons. Thus, even before the war, relatively few young Germans came to America to start a new life. Almost all German-Americans are real Americans, born in America as the second or even the third generation. This fact is emphasized by German-Americans everywhere; I found when I talked with them that in most cases their grandparents or their father or mother had come from Germany; many of them were not purely of German blood; their ancestors had intermarried with other nationalities. As a matter of fact there are now very few German-Americans who were born in Germany. Those who are left are usually men or women of sixty-odd years, who have spent most of their lives, and in many cases most of their childhood, in America, and who have been American citizens for decades. Many of the older people, and most of the younger generation, are entirely Americanized, especially when they have acquired wealth, a leading social position or when they have become important in American public life. Others, who still cling to their German traditions and customs, frequently joined some exclusively German group early in life. Their knowledge of the "Wilhelmian" Germany, which as a rule is based on short visits, is superficial only. Most of them, though still attached to the democratic ideas of the 1848 Revolution, are the good reliable "Bürger" so typical in Germany during the eighties, in Bismarck's Germany from which they emigrated. They are industrious, conscientious and entirely reliable in their narrow spheres; they will not set the world on fire, but they command their fellow citizens' respect by their devotion to small tasks and duties and by their desire to do their best. In public life their activities have been similar; a firm political will to achieve great things was not characteristic of these immigrants who came from a state as authoritative as Germany. Public-minded efforts towards small aims, towards tangible ends, were more suited to their modest, capable natures. Their interests consisted in organizing German hospitals, German learned societies and German "vereins" generally, where they could feel at home. They were especially fond of their athletic clubs, their "turnvereins," and their singing clubs, "gesangvereins."

It must be remembered, however, that before the war, the difference between the two types of German-Americans, thoroughly Americanized Germans on the one hand and presidents of turnvereins on the other, was not as great as it might seem. Americanized Germans had not, after all, weakly surrendered their innate national characteristics. These people had become Americanized more quickly, that is all; they had intermingled more rapidly with the other nationalities living in America. This does not mean that they were merely absorbed by any other race; on the contrary they coöperated with the others in the creation of this new nation—America. German-Americans contributed their traditions as equally valid parts to this new creation. Their contribution is apparent in all phases of American life.

The members of the "Vereins" also considered themselves as real Americans, as Americans of German descent, who wanted to retain the cultural values they had brought with them from the old country. But it was as Americans that they consciously aimed to instill their traditions and customs, the best they had to give, into their new home. This was their contribution to America, which, as equals, they wanted to help create.

Both types of German-Americans could not, in the long run, withstand the melting pot's most potent factor: the English language. Even in families belonging to the "Vereine" the younger generation grew away from the German language; inevitably they associated increasingly with people of other nationalities. Regular immigration from Germany stopped in the nineties. New Germans no longer came to keep alive these traditions and so in the natural course of events, German-Americans were predestined to be assimilated into America's population as a whole.

The conflict came in 1914 when war began; and

it was brought to a head when America entered the war.

"Yes, had we been like the Irish," many German-Americans claim, "if we like them had thrown our political influence into the balance—America would never have entered the war, for the people wanted to stay out. Wilson had been elected a second time because he promised to keep the country out of war. It was like a slap in the face, shortly after the election, when under pressure from England and especially from Wall Street, he declared war anyway, for we did not know what was going on. At that time there was no real war sentiment, it had to be created artificially later on."

I heard statements of this kind again and again and with them bitter complaints about those German-Americans who, when there was still time, were not courageous or spirited enough to make material sacrifices to counteract British-French propaganda and thus to prevent the threatening disaster. I prefer to recall those who suffered an intense inner conflict throughout these years and who nevertheless remained true to themselves.

"Our situation was terrible and in many ways it is difficult even to-day. Neither here nor in Germany were we understood, nor do people want to understand us. Here we are suspected of being traitors and in Germany we are considered deserters. In reality we are neither one nor the other. We are of German descent, but we are Americans. Most of us were born here and the rest have at any rate dedicated their whole lives to this country. We love our German ancestry and what it stands for, but we love this country, which is our home, our state; we cannot imagine living anywhere but in America. We are and want to be citizens of this country—full-fledged, not second-rate, citizens; we do not want to be citizens with any 'hyphen.' When war was declared our sons were drafted into the army. What else could they have done? And when the critical moment came, what else could we, as responsible citizens, have done but to do our duty by our country? This does not mean that we betrayed our German ancestry; on the contrary we have suffered a great deal for it."

This is what they say and they tell the truth. It is a fact that German-Americans who admitted their ancestry—as a contrast to others who, to maintain their position, were more patriotic than the patriots, and many of whom, even to-day, talk in terms of a 100 per cent Americanism—have suffered profoundly for many years. During the war excitement they were persecuted as German sympathizers; every word they uttered was spied upon. Official propagandists, and especially the newspapers, tried again and again to force them to state that either they would repudiate their German traditions or give themselves up to the Department of Justice. They were excluded from clubs, from social connections generally. Their social position was undermined, an attempt was made to ruin their business, in fact these German-Americans suffered all kinds of brutal terror, including terroristic court decisions and bodily injuries.

Family quarrels, differences with their children or with friends, all tended to increase their bitterness. Then came the German breakdown which many of them had considered inevitable all along. The laborious and painful reconstruction period in the new Germany followed, which many of the German-

Americans could not understand. But they did understand the suffering which came with the collapse of the former Empire and now, at least, they could help. Even their efforts in this direction were not always easy, for now they were often misunderstood in their old home. During the inflation period in Germany it frequently happened that people preferred to accept outside help rather than to make an intense effort themselves. Many Germans considered every American a millionaire, and even if he gave a great deal it never seemed enough. The German-Americans who were the first to help suffering Germans in the old country, were, however, very rarely millionaires. On the contrary most of them were hard-working people, who had themselves lost a great deal during the war. In fact often they were more generous than they could really afford to be. They even worked harder, so that they could give more. Even as late as the spring of 1925 groups of German-American women, organized after the war, met once a week in a number of American cities and devoted a full eight-hour day to making dresses and undergarments for suffering German children. The hands and faces of these women showed that they had plenty of regular sewing and housework to do as it was. Nevertheless, they have been willing for six years to give the strength of their spirit and the labor of their hands to poor German children. We can do nothing but bow our heads in gratitude for so much kindness. . . .

The situation of German-Americans has improved, as the war has become more and more an event of the past, and many Americans themselves are wishing that the war-time persecution of these people, which is now a painful memory, might sink into oblivion. New connections are being established and the respect they formerly enjoyed is being re-awakened. Post-war emigration from Germany has, in fact, somewhat increased the number of Germans in the United States, but nevertheless the harm done during the war is immeasurable. This fact is clearly reflected in the way in which the German language is losing ground. German, which was extensively taught in American schools before the United States entered the war, was stopped entirely in many States afterwards, partly because the pupils, including children of German descent, refused to learn it, and partly because German was simply abolished by influential people. This will continue to be a great loss in the future, for to-day, even in states with a large German-American population, German is being taught only to a limited extent in the schools. In the colleges and universities, as well, instruction in German language and literature, formerly very popular subjects, was decreased enormously during the war. Now these subjects are becoming gradually more important in the college curricula, but they are not nearly as popular as they were before the war. German newspapers, the circulation of which could be kept alive during the war only by publishing them in English, are also losing ground all the time.

This decrease in the use of German would doubtless have occurred even had there been no war, but then the process would have occurred more slowly; it would have been coördinated with the gradual growing together of the population as a whole. The abrupt termination of this German influence through the war meant the destruction of a valuable cultural factor in American life.

The English elements have gained the influence which the Germans have lost since 1914. Tradition, language and finance are the three mighty pillars of British prestige in America. A German visiting in the United States is often asked why Germany so underestimated England's influence in America during the war, especially as this influence was increased by British propaganda on a huge scale. "As soon as England seemed seriously threatened it was quite certain that America would enter the war, and if England were in distress to-morrow America would doubtless come to the rescue again, despite all the differences separating the two countries." This statement, made by a clever man, may be somewhat counteracted by what I was told by another: "We participated in one European war and we had enough. The American people will not take part in a second war in Europe." There are unquestionably many people who share this peaceful assurance, but the lesson contained in the first statement quoted should nevertheless not be overlooked or forgotten.

England and the United States were separated by as important an event as America's independence, when the thirteen colonies, through their Declaration of Independence, on July 4, 1776, repudiated British rule and won their freedom in the War of 1775-83. Since then the Fourth of July has been the United States' great national holiday: history taught in the schools and the historical traditions of America's freedom are directed against England. Practically, however, the consciousness of this fact is passing and the World War has hastened this change.

It is not necessary here to mention individuals who from 1914-19 preached enthusiastically that all the events leading up to 1776 were really caused by

the "German" (or even "Prussian") King George
III of England, for all kinds of nonsense was
preached during the war in every country. It is a
more important consideration that a feeling of alliance between the United States and England is now
being systematically encouraged. This feeling has
become so general that some Americans (and they
are not German-Americans either) complain angrily
that a part of the New Englanders seem to consider
the Revolution and the War of Independence as
merely an internal British affair, and the United
States as a Dominion of the British Empire.

High finance as represented by the largest banking
houses in New York is the strongest influence working towards closer relations between the two countries. The powerful financial interests in New York
and London constantly coöperate in political and
economic decisions. These financial circles in New
York, in turn, are in close touch with Washington,
which is the political center of the country and the
seat of Congress and the Federal Government. It
is rather extensively believed that these financiers
ultimately caused America to enter the war, which
reflects Wall Street's connection with Washington.
According to this view Wilson had to declare war
on Germany when the Morgan banks and their associates had gone the limit in granting loans to the
Allies. When they were not able to issue further
loans, they felt uneasy about the ones already
granted. It is said, furthermore, that when war
was declared the United States Treasury took over
these Morgan loans, and these anglophile bankers in
New York were relieved of their worry.

Doubtless financial circles could not exercise so
great a political influence if Anglo-American rela-

tions, which they cultivate, were not supported in any case by the predominant prestige enjoyed by the descendants of English immigrants in the East, and by the tenaciousness with which they cling to their British traditions and customs. The awe of English society is not unimportant either; an English lord is, after all, the highest ideal of the flappers of America's financial aristocracy. (In the same way the ribbon of the French Legion of Honor is a French propaganda medium not to be underestimated in America, where there are no national orders.)

It is an even more important consideration that America has derived her modes of life from England. America's homes are English, and so are her clubs and sports. But the decisive factor lies even deeper: it is based on the great ethical-religious traditions which were brought to the new country by English Puritanism and English Quakerdom. These traditions first came to America with people who were struggling against the reigning powers in the homes from which they had fled. These ideas, and the conception of political liberty and democratic self-government which they implied, became the fundamental principles upon which American life was based. The influence of these traditions of thought, given by one race of immigrants to all the rest like a dowry, is constantly winning friends for England. The tremendous, binding force of the common language is another important factor. Even in science this is evident, for in every field of scientific endeavor so much has been written in English, that only a small number of scientists in America consider it necessary regularly to read books or articles published in other languages. As far as the press is concerned conditions are similar: English newspapers, English news agencies, English opinion generally, exercise almost complete control. And the people themselves? Even at school they read an English Bible, English poets, they read English history about British heroes. Is it surprising, therefore, that the British consider that American life developing in this new country is more or less only a modification of British life?

Anglo-American influence dominates so completely only in the East. For just as there are three economic areas, the United States is really subdivided into three different areas as far as the customs and the modes of life of the people are concerned. (I am not including the South, which I did not visit, in this discussion.)

In the East, where people look towards Europe, the population is attached to England, as its great example. In the West, where great developments are only beginning, the inhabitants of the few large port cities are more interested in what is happening on the other side of the Pacific than across the Atlantic. Only in special cases when, for instance, people hear that the same anxiety concerning Japanese immigration, which troubles them, is worrying Canadians or Australians do they feel a bond with the British Empire.

Between the East and the West, between the two mountain regions stretching from North to South, is the Middle West, the part of the country which is becoming an increasingly important center for the intellectual and political as well as for the economic progress of the country as a whole. . . . A European diplomat who really knows the United States indicated the importance of the Middle West very clearly. All great European powers, he said, made a mistake during the war by not taking the Middle West into consideration. The English were wrong when they thought that America would declare war at once. Germany made a mistake the other way around, because she thought the United States would never enter the war; France was wrong when she believed that America would ratify the Treaty of Versailles—all these powers misjudged the Middle West which in each case proved to be the decisive factor.

For in the huge Mississippi Valley, in this "valley of democracy," where in a way colonization is so much younger than in the East, and yet where, in other ways, it is more mature than in the Far West, here in the Middle West, where various European races have intermingled most completely without the historical predominance of one nation, as in the East, "a new type of individual, the American type, a new people, the American people, is developing."

AMERICA'S PUBLIC LIFE

To understand the world in which the American, especially the average Middle Western American, lives, it must be remembered how lonely and sparsely populated this country is, and how relatively young is its colonization. It must be remembered also how prosperous the majority of Americans are. They are citizens of a continent, but their lives and their minds are really attuned to a narrow circle. The American lives in his family and his home, on his farm or for his business, and on that basis in his community, in his town, with which he grows and develops. His immediate environment constitutes his world and here his tasks are simple and his aims are tangible. His pride and ambition are satisfied in this narrow circle, where his sense of service is appealed to.

"We are an extremely provincial people," Americans admit and they are right. American cities may be huge, but they are not the less provincial. A population of a hundred million may imply as many provincials. Patriots, but, in practice, their patriotism is primarily local patriotism. The object of their devotion must change frequently, for they move so often from town to town. They are, however, able to transfer their local patriotism from one narrow circle to another just as easily as they move from one state, or one city to another.

This provincialism received its first shock during the war; for the first time people realized how closely connected they were, after all, with the outside world, and to what an extent they depended upon it, especially from an economic point of view, about which they were especially sensitive, but their understanding went no further.

"It was terrible that we were drawn into the war," a remarkable American woman said to me, "particularly as we did not feel its full moral effect: we suffered too little, we were too far away from it all, we always lagged a step behind Europe's experiences, so that even to-day our people do not really know what war means. But if we had kept out of it altogether it would have been fatal too, in one sense, for then we would now have no understanding whatsoever for the rest of the world."

As it is most Americans have little understanding for the rest of the world, in general and for Europe in particular. "From Seattle to Chemnitz is exactly the same distance as from Chemnitz to Seattle;" the western part of America is separated from Europe by a continent and an ocean, but the Middle West, which is several days by train away from either ocean, seems even farther away. In New York a few large newspapers maintain a regular foreign correspondence, but as one travels inland, the European news printed in the papers becomes shorter, more disconnected and more unreliable. At every stopping place on a journey West, news from Europe seems to move farther away from the front page, and local murders, accidents, robberies, baseball or football and small society events seem to become more important. A few isolated papers, attempting to handle a better service, seem to be the exception proving the rule.

The type of news generally published is very symptomatic of American life: the newspapers publish what the people want, and the public, extremely provincial indeed, feels no interest in Europe worth mentioning. Before the war perhaps only large export trades, such as the steel and oil industries, and foreign trade firms in general, were interested in developments abroad; even the interest of the banks, aside from a few New York houses, were chiefly local, provincial. Now large investment houses, issuing foreign loans, are trying to create markets in the West and in the Middle West as well as in the East, and they are advertising Europe with considerable intelligence. But this has not as yet resulted in any profound understanding of Europe; many of the best and most sincere types of Americans were discouraged by their war experiences from having much to do with Europe. In so far as they were overwhelmed by war propaganda at all, they really thought that the United States entered the war for idealistic reasons. Wilson's failure during the peace negotiations in Paris meant a complete disillusionment for these believing, sincerely idealistic people. Subsequent events in Europe, from the Versailles Treaty to the occupation of the Ruhr, strengthened them in their belief that the best and most sensible thing America could do in future was to have as little as possible to do with Europe. They want European debtor nations to pay their debts, for they do not see why American taxpayers should be lenient, if the countries involved use the money, which America has let them have, only to increase their military armaments, so that they can continue to ruin Europe by their policy of force and endanger the peace of the world. Besides these people do not see why the United States should be involved in European affairs; they want America to keep aloof

—because of this attitude they disapproved of the United States signing the Peace Treaty. They demanded that American troops should be withdrawn from the Rhineland, they demanded that America should not become a member of the League of Nations, and that the United States keep out of Europe's quarrels. This point of view was so general that Congress could not allocate government funds to the Dawes Committee; the Committee was in fact not sent to Europe officially, and the funds necessary for the Committee were furnished privately.

In the East a different attitude prevails. Here people might more readily approve of America's assisting Europe during her reconstruction period, as well as America's entrance into the League. Both these aims might be brought about as a result of America's coöperation with England. But the Middle West wants to keep out of European affairs and it is the Middle West which exerts the decisive influence.

Middle Western policy of non-interference has two very different causes. On the one hand it is based on the narrow provincial viewpoint which prevails there: people know nothing about Europe and care less. There is so much to do at home. Mrs. Carol Kennicott must beautify Gopher Prairie's Main Street; and Zenith, Mr. Babbitt's excellent city, must lead the trade not only in condensed milk and cream, in cardboard boxes and lamps, but in cheese, leather goods, roofing felt, foodstuffs and overalls as well.

Middle Western policy of isolation is, on the other hand, based on entirely conscientious reasoning shared by many idealists, who feel that they were abused during the war and who do not want this to happen again. New York's opposition to this isolation policy only makes Middle Westerners all the more suspicious. When asked whether they really believe that the largest and wealthiest country in the world should never assume its share in the responsibility of shaping the fate of the world and the future of humanity, they shrug their shoulders in resignation. "What do you want us to do?" they ask. "We simply have not the means to assume this responsibility. Even were we to enter the League, and it were thus to become a real League of Nations, we should never be sure how our representatives in Geneva would act, for the good are powerless and the powerful are bad."

As a matter of fact this policy of negation has not been quite negative in its influence: because of it America got out of the military alliance with France, America took an increasingly decisive stand against Poincaré's policy of force and refused to help him by canceling France's debts. This American point of view undoubtedly encouraged France to change her attitude. Any creditor can tighten or loosen his hold on his debtors or any wealthy man can grant or refuse credits as he pleases, and thus America's policy has undoubtedly been an important factor in helping maintain the peace of Europe at least in this point. Middle Western adherents of the isolation policy agree with Eastern anglophiles. But for Middle Westerners this pacifistic influence is only a secondary consideration.

A few people in this part of the country, however, would approve of America's entrance into the League, where, they believe, she should work actively towards the establishment of world democracy, but they are isolated. Others, too, may change their views about the League if the Locarno Conference results in a real European peace. But it is a mistake to believe that America as a whole will look towards Europe intensively in the immediate future. This can happen only when the Middle West has become sufficiently mature. But here at present the distrust of Europe is deeply rooted. The tendency towards isolation is even more deeply rooted. A provincialism, concentrating the people's complete attention on their small immediate circle, on their small, immediate tasks, is even more firmly rooted among the masses of people, though not among the small group of intellectual idealists, in the Middle West.

Except in the East, therefore, the great problems concerning the future of the world are not the center of interest in American life. Even questions concerning America's own internal politics are not, generally speaking, considered to be of prime importance. It must be considered in advance that the fundamental principles of the state and of the Constitution are common property of the whole people, and are outside the struggle, not even to be discussed. Not only the Republic, but also the democracy, "the government of the people, by the people, for the people," is deeply rooted in the people's history and faith. These basic principles are a part of the air Americans breathe; it is unthinkable that any individual, any group of people or any party, would openly attack them. And it should be remembered that this democracy is not fictitious. Despite the great powers of the President, for instance, it would be impossible for him, just as it is for Congress, to adopt any policy against the will of the people. Any one wanting to put through political measures must have, or win, the support of the people before he can succeed. The politicians' ears are always close to the ground, as the saying goes; they are in constant touch with the people whose attitude and desires they wish to understand at once.

But to-day Americans are not, broadly speaking, confronted with any great, stirring problems affecting them profoundly as a people which they should endeavor to solve through political measures or through legislation. The voters as a whole are chiefly concerned with a desire to maintain the present state of prosperity and all other aims are subordinate to this one.

For this reason America is to-day probably the most conservative country in the world. Any one suspected of wanting to endanger the present order by force is forcefully removed from the political arena, for in this point political struggles are as brutal as social ones. Even to-day, seven years after the war, there are men in American prisons who were sentenced by the Draconian war regulations, because they opposed the interests of the state— perhaps some of them did nothing worse than openly to proclaim convictions which were not in accord with the popular war sentiment. America is the only country participating in the war which has not granted amnesty to her political prisoners. And why should she do so? Public opinion in the United States is not in the least concerned either with these prisoners or with terroristic sentences which have been handed down since the end of the war; after all most people consider these prisoners as anarchists, syndicalists, communists or bolshevists. The war was considered an excellent opportunity of getting rid of them for a while at least. For above all:

prosperity shall not be threatened. The extent to which this attitude is influencing America's politics, —how, in practice, it prevents the development of a strong political will in this country,—was indicated by La Follette's overwhelming defeat in the last presidential elections.

For La Follette, whom public opinion in America considered a radical, was really only a sincere believer in democracy. He wanted to preserve the democratic ideals of the American Constitution, even where party machines or vested interests were concerned. All his life he fought against these two elements, which are adulterating American democracy. In his own state, where he made these "Wisconsin ideas" victorious, he brought the big railroad companies more or less under the control of the state; he introduced a progressive and fair system of taxation; he imbued legislation with social ideals. He broke the autocracy and party bosses lost their power. Many democratic reforms, adopted during the last few decades by a number of individual states, originated in Wisconsin, La Follette's model state. But in the presidential election he was overwhelmingly defeated. He was supported by only a relatively small number of newspapers; only small funds were available for his campaign and the great vested interests fought him with all the powers at their command. In some plants the workers were dismissed just before the elections and they were told that they would be reinstated if the official Republican candidate was elected, but that the factory would shut down if La Follette were victorious. A number of banks exerted the same kind of pressure by telling the rural population that the rates of interest on mortgages would be increased or that mortgages would be recalled if Coolidge were not elected. The New York Stock Exchange lowered quotation rates after huge crowds had attended an election speech of La Follette's in the city. The election slogan of the official Republican Party simply proclaimed that prosperity was guaranteed if Coolidge were elected, but that it was endangered if he were defeated. All kinds of pressure was exerted to emphasize this slogan. But what is most significant is the fact that these methods were so successful. After all ballotting is secret, and if, nevertheless, only a small percentage of workers, who at first strongly favored La Follette, voted for him, if the farmers, among whom he had at first had many followers, were influenced against him because grain prices rose just before the elections, it indicates to what an extent the political wishes of even these classes of voters are subject to an even greater desire: that prosperity may not be interrupted.

The party system in America can only be understood if this lack of any great political tasks or aims is taken into consideration. Officially, as is well known, there are two parties, the Republicans and the Democrats, who fight against each other for power. But it is a useless task to try to discover any real differences between them. "The Democrats believe that the government is rotten when the Republicans are in power, and the Republicans believe the same when the Democrats are in control and the few Socialists believe that every government is rotten"—this humorous interpretation of the different platforms is, indeed, very near the truth.

Both parties are historical developments; the geographic areas where either of them controls the vote are historical as well and only in rare cases

when an outstanding personality, like Roosevelt or
Wilson, is involved do they endanger each other's
territories.   Both parties are old and old-fashioned,
and in view of the present attitude there is no room
for a new party.   All efforts to organize a third
party have so far failed at the very beginning; they
have been partially successful only in one or another
state.   But no third party has recently had any influence on politics as a whole; a will to make decisions, appealing aims and leaders are lacking.
Even a man like La Follette for years did not dare
to oppose the Grand Old Party by founding a new
one.   He always fought inside the Republican
Party, to reform it from within.

The idea of a Labor Party plays a certain rôle
among the younger, and more radical, sections of
the labor movement, but it is out of the question that
such a party will develop in the immediate future,
that is to say while prosperity continues.   So far
the idea of a Labor Party is discussed only by small
groups of people with no will to act.   The leaders
and the masses among the membership of the A. F.
of L. oppose a Labor Party strenuously.   On every
possible occasion the Federation emphasizes its nonpartisan character and the fact that it is neutral as
far as all parties are concerned.   Once when a
foreign visitor mentioned the British Labor Party to
Gompers he answered in a deprecatory fashion:
"Yes, the English spend their time on politics, but
what we want is to fight for higher wages," and
the Federation's attitude has not changed since his
death.

The Federation does not believe in the power of
a new party to divide the older ones according to
new principles.   The Federation does not believe in

this vitality or this strength, because it does not feel
them within its own organization and because it does
not even consider the political aims which such a
party would involve, and consequently the A. F. of
L. does not think that such a party would be possible.
On the contrary, the Federation tries to benefit from
its nonpartisan, neutral position and to realize its
own immediate desires. The Federation aims to use
the influence made possible by the Democratic ballot
by influencing both Republicans and Democrats, first
the nominees and later the successful candidates
themselves.

It is customary before elections for labor organizations to present a list of requests to the candidates : the one promising to grant the greatest number of these requests is recommended to the union
membership's vote, no matter to which party he belongs. In some cases this system has been greatly
perfected; certain trade union headquarters keep
exact records of the way each member of each legislative body voted in issues concerning which the
unions took a definite stand. Toward the end of the
campaigns these records are published : Senator A.
of the Democratic Party voted twenty-three times
the right way and never the wrong way, though once
he was absent. Senator B. of the Republican Party
was almost as well behaved; once he was absent
when the votes were cast, but twenty-one times he
voted right and twice wrong. Senator Z., on the
other hand, also of the Republican Party, is the bad
man on the list of candidates, for he voted the
wrong way twenty-four times. When such statistics
are published before each election, the members of
the union are won for the reëlection of Mr. A. and
Mr. B., but against the election and even the nomi-

nation of Mr. Z., and through the labor press and union meetings a larger circle of voters is influenced. Some women's organizations take a similar stand. The finest people everywhere who are not attracted by either of the two parties realize how little they can do against these powerful machines from within, so they try to influence them from without.

Big Business interests exert the greatest influence on both parties and on politics as a whole. Like the labor unions, and many idealistic women, they are fundamentally nonpartisan and do not vote for party candidates as such, but for specific candidates of either party who may be most useful to them. Big Business contributes to the campaign funds of both parties, so that as many candidates who will be useful to business as possible may be elected, regardless of their party affiliations. Big Business has representatives and confidants in both parties,—the influence of vested interests is far-reaching; it extends into the city councils, into Congress, into administrative offices everywhere.

A leading citizen who is close to these interests said to me: "One can't really say that the wealthy rule in this country, but it is undoubtedly true that they exert a controlling influence in many cases. And this is not undemocratic, for in this country the people have faith in the wealthy and believe in their leaderships, for the wealthy have already attained the success which every one hopes to attain himself: so the people believe that if these successful and wealthy men lead them all will be well."

This interpretation of plutocracy is certainly rosy, too rosy, but there is nevertheless some truth in what he said. True, it is now a few decades since successful business men were worshiped as creators

by the people's imagination, and since the building of
the great transcontinental railroads was spoken of
as achievements as "great as Napoleon's campaigns."
Successful speculations on the stock market do not,
as a rule, call forth such admiration. But it is
nevertheless true that Americans feel great respect
for successful business men, a respect undoubtedly
based on Calvinistic doctrines. And if one looks
attentively for the factors which are influencing and
directing public opinion, one finds again and again
many successful business men. The other side of
the picture, however, is equally and terrifyingly evident: the business atmosphere permeates or even
corrupts many men active in public life.

With few exceptions newspapers are commercialized, and the press is an enterprise like any
other; the newspapers deal in news just as other
concerns deal in iron or cotton. The business managers, and not the editors, determine the contents
and the attitudes of their papers, and they manage
them to suit the business interests involved. It is
undoubtedly untrue that, as was frequently believed
in Germany, English or French capital bought out
American papers during the war. The American
press is so wealthy that it does not need subsidies
of this kind. The majority of them are managed
from a business point of view, and a large circulation and a large number of advertisers is the great
aim of American newspapers.

"A newspaper's success," the publisher of a
medium-sized paper in a medium-sized city explained
to me, "means its circulation, which, in turn, determines the amount of advertising space which is
bought, and the public will not read papers that have
no advertisements. For the women, especially, they

are more important than the editorials. It is therefore customary to print the editorial columns somewhere on a page near the back of American papers. Investigation has proved that only 5 per cent of the readers pay any attention to the editorial page. In my paper, therefore we consider editorials unimportant; we buy them ready to print from some syndicate—all other items are more important."

Not all, but most, newspapers in the United States are manufactured this way and their influence on public opinion is evaluated accordingly, that is to say they have no political leadership at all. But by a suggestive selection and a suggestive make-up of the news this commercialized press can, at times, exert a devastating influence on its uncritical readers and the commercialized press, furthermore, tends to make the public shallow and superficial by publishing long accounts of professional sporting events and the activities of innumerable lodges, clubs, societies and organizations. By giving so much space to these small, trivial events, most American papers cause their readers to consider them important. These American papers are demoralizing, furthermore, through their brutal and sometimes terroristic accounts of people's private affairs. This kind of reporting humors the reading public and the press lends itself to it because it means good business. These newspapers harbor no ambition to have political leadership, which they could not have in any case, since they have no moral authority.

The majority of politicians as well have no moral authority. Only a few are believed to be fighting for an idea. Public opinion considers most politicians as business men whose business is politics, who, if all goes well, expect to get a job or a position out of their politics and who, if worse comes to the worst, are accessible to actual corruption. A great deal of corruption has undoubtedly been rooted out during the last decades, but the memory of the havoc caused by this evil in Congress and State Assemblies, in administrative offices and even in labor unions, keeps people suspicious. Even administrative officers who are actually elected are sometimes distrusted; at best they are respected as able administrators, but never as representative leaders of the people. City halls, therefore, are merely office buildings of various sizes, and not the city's intellectual centers. They are administrative offices and not the pulse of the community. For this reason there are no formal reception rooms in these city halls: if the citizens want to receive visitors they can do so in clubs or hotels, and it is not the mayor but the big business men who give these receptions. This is typical of American life.

Quite incidentally, in "Twenty Years at Hull House," Jane Addams describes her impressions of the Passion Play which she saw at Oberammergau in 1900. The old Gospel story was brought home to her as something real and vital by the peasants' simple acting. As she listened to them she became thoughtful. "They made clear," she writes, "that the opposition to the young Teacher sprang from the merchants whose traffic in the temple He had disturbed and from the Pharisees who were dependent upon them for support. Their query was curiously familiar, as they demanded the antecedents of the Radical who dared to touch vested interests, who presumed to dictate the morality of trade, and who insulted the marts of honest merchants by calling them 'a den of thieves.' As the play developed, it became clear that this powerful opposition had friends in Church and State, that they controlled influences which ramified in all directions. They obviously believed in their statement of the case and their very wealth and position in the community gave their words such weight that finally all of their hearers were convinced that the young Agitator must be done away with in order that the highest interests of society might be conserved. These simple peasants made it clear that it was the money power which induced one of the Agitator's closest friends to betray him, and the villain of the piece, Judas himself, was only a man who was so dazzled by money, so under the domination of all it represented, that he was perpetually blind to the spiritual vision unrolling before him."

The influence of money and of people who own it on public life, administrative bodies and on the thoughts and attitudes of the people themselves, who "believe in the wealthy," can not be more clearly described than by the simple words of this clear-sighted woman who, in the Passion Play at Oberammergau, recognized point by point the political forces at work in her own country. In his memoirs La Follette practically confirms these observations.

The country is too prosperous—is the explanation I heard again and again for the meagerness of America's public life. The country is too prosperous; therefore politics is not in the center of the thoughts and feelings of the people. The country is too prosperous: America has no frontiers threatened from the outside, there are no problems of foreign policy which really matter—the people are not educated by need to consider international affairs. America is too prosperous: therefore vital, social problems have not developed, the outward and visible stability of her democratic institutions has caused America to overlook the forces which are corrupting her from within and specific political issues do not seem urgent to the people as a whole—there is no suffering which makes it imperative for them to cultivate a political will.

Graft? "Why, yes, there is some graft, but it only makes our administration a little more expensive and we are rich enough to bear the costs." Exploitation of others by big business? "Why, yes, probably to a certain extent, but we are rich enough to be exploited a little." Is the cost of living increased by the high protective tariff? "Certainly, all economists in America agree in condemning high duties, but—the country is too prosperous."

It is a fact, the country is too prosperous. Its spaciousness and the youth of its colonization offer every one so many opportunities, there is so much to do for every one, that it seems only natural for each individual to concentrate on his particular activity. This concentration means the best service for the nation as a whole. Provincialism and local patriotism are always characteristic of pioneers and of colonials. The country as a whole will progress in any case; America is blooming and does not need to worry about a few blemishes. If his country calls him, even a provincial American will follow the call, that is, if it is sufficiently persuasive and thrilling.

For despite everything America is not a country of crass, flat materialism. Doubtless there is such materialism—just as, God knows, there is some in Germany—and the war and war profiteering and post-war prosperity have undoubtedly encouraged it. This period decreased the American people's morale —just as it affected people in other countries—and stimulated cynicism, frivolity and brutality. Above all the greater the chances of making money the greater became the lust for money. The more accessible material pleasure became the greater grew the effort to attain it. The greater prosperity, the more people were afraid of endangering it. All this seems very clear and it sufficiently explains a part of the American people, just as it explains some of the people in every other country. This also explains why labor, an important fact in American public life, may not be considered simply as a group fighting for progress as it is in the industrial countries of Western and Central Europe. It must be remembered in this connection that American labor does not consider itself as a special and permanent class, a class which has to develop special class ideas from such permanent class differences.

Labor in America simply includes those people who are just beginning to try to realize their material aims, and who more than others for this reason feel obliged to concentrate all their efforts, their strength and their thoughts, on these aims. It is particularly labor, therefore, which lacks the courage, and the liberty, to consider questions beyond and outside immediate personal issues. Besides, as soon as labor has left the "scum," it becomes a part of America as a whole, it is not separated from the rest by class barriers, and so the workers are just as materialistic or just as idealistic as their other fellow citizens.

It is true that Americans generally are not "thinkers and poets." They are people who attack things practically and who act in a pragmatic manner. Despite this fact many of them have retained what is most important—political faith. Many Americans, with their uncomplicated simplicity, are not "too clever" to believe in democracy, they are not "too highly educated" to believe in political freedom, they are not "too skeptical" to believe in political ideals in general. They believe in the value of democracy and liberalism, they believe in the ultimate aims of right and justice, as they understand them. And because they are believers, they are if necessary willing to make sacrifices. The capacity for belief and sacrifice can be abused as was shown by America's entrance into the war. The danger of such abuse is greater now than it was, because wartime propaganda developed demagogy to the highest degree, and the large vested interests learned how to influence public opinion to an alarming extent.

America's entrance into the war does not, however, discredit the American people as such. For they believed—as the people of all the other nations did—that the reasons for the war were pure and unselfish and so they were willing to sacrifice themselves. Americans are innately capable of so much faith and such great sacrifices, even during periods when they are not called upon by their leaders to prove it, when they are not made conscious of their faith and their spirit of sacrifice. This is the case at present. When the country is "too prosperous" materialism is powerful because the people do not quite know what to do with their power and with their money. But as they always realize that everything which has been achieved and created has resulted from the strength and the will of the people themselves and not from a command of some monarch—one day the apathy of the people may again disappear, just as it did when

Roosevelt or Wilson summoned them to fight for some vital issue affecting their liberty, for democracy as against the great vested interests. In times like the present America's idealism is latent, but the decisive fact remains that this idealism does exist among great masses of the people, that the faith in democracy is alive even in times like the present. And that means a great deal.

PRIVATE LIFE AND SOCIAL FORCES IN AMERICA

In a small town, about an hour by train from New York, I visited friends in their country home, where they live in peace and quiet, close to nature and far away from the noise of the great city. Unless some one comes from New York to see them they live a solitary life in the town, which my friend's wife seldom leaves. They know no one; they do not associate with any other family in the town. And why is this? They are Lutherans; there are two other Christian communities in the place, but no Lutheran Church which they might have joined—and so they are isolated and separated from all social intercourse. This is not an exceptional case; it is typical of conditions in many large and small towns in America.

The churches are the most important social centers in America. In small communities there is no other opportunity for sociability. Usually a town has several churches, belonging to various creeds and sects, which compete with each other most strenuously. In a town with a population of ten thousand inhabitants which I visited, there are ten churches competing for the greatest membership. A newcomer to the town, who decides which church he will attend, must determine, at the same time, with which circle of people he wants to associate. If for some reason or other he does not join any church he can have no friends or social ties and will remain an outsider.

In large cities church life is, of course, not so important, but many people attend divine service every Sunday morning as a matter of course. I cannot judge how far-reaching church membership is in the United States, nor from what sections of the population this membership is generally recruited, but I can state that I saw crowded Protestant churches on fashionable Fifth Avenue as well as in the workers' district in Chicago. I know, furthermore, that in a university town like Madison students of both sexes go to church regularly. I was told that many of them, belonging to the Unitarian church, where all kinds of humanitarian and social problems are discussed from the pulpit, follow the minister far more attentively than they do their university professors. During my travels in America I met a number of Protestant ministers, chiefly liberals, and none of them complained about a lack of interest in the churches.

This support of the church in a country where church and state are entirely separated interested me very much. Religion is not taught in the public schools, but a number of churches have solved this problem by giving the children daily religious instruction during the weeks before school is reopened in the fall. The attendance on these classes, which occupy as much time as regular school work, is entirely optional, and just for this reason, perhaps, the children are glad to take part.

The state does not contribute one cent towards the support of the churches; there are no obligatory church taxes in America, where the churches are supported by voluntary contributions. It is only natural, therefore, that some of them are financially dependent upon their wealthy members, and this dependency is not very favorable to the undiluted Word of God; but, on the other hand, this voluntary support stimulates the people to serve and to help in their community. I had occasion to study this development in a small Middle Western town, where, under the auspices of the Chamber of Commerce, a simple public dinner is given every month, attended by more than three hundred people, including representatives of every organization in the city, from the college president to a delegate from the local association of stenographers. These dinners begin with a prayer; then, first patriotic and later humorous songs are sung by all those present, after which current municipal problems are discussed. The evening closes with an address by some out-of-town speaker. The dinner itself is prepared and served by the women's church organizations, each in their turn. Women of all classes of society voluntarily take part in this work (which, of course, does not hurt their social prestige, for every kind of work is respected in America) and they are glad to earn a small profit from the dinner for the benefit of their church. And it seems to me that ministers with whom I discussed the problem are right when they base the great moral influence of the churches on their voluntary membership and voluntary contributions and the fact that they are quite independent of the state. As a result of this system the churches are institutions which really belong to their members, who pay their minister to tell them the truth and who respect him for doing it.

To a German these church organizations seem very strange at first. I met a young minister of a church with fifteen hundred members, for instance, who has a regular office, an assistant and three stenographers whose typewriters click incessantly, right in a new Gothic church building. His administrative duties are extensive. The annual budget of this particular church community amounts to $50,-000; the minister's salary is $6,000 and an automobile, which the church rents for him, and which, of course, he drives himself. Divine Service and Sunday school, for children of various ages, are not the only activities of this church, which serves as a regular meeting place for its members, and all kinds of problems are discussed with the minister at these gatherings. Even church members, like the ones included in this community, are organized into clubs (men's clubs and women's clubs, clubs for young people and clubs for small boys and girls), with special functions and activities. A news sheet, published weekly by the minister, keeps the members in touch with events in their community.

The work of many churches is even more far-reaching. Some churches have gymnasiums where dances are given frequently, for, as the argument goes, young people will dance in any case, so it is better for them to do so where they can be watched by the minister and their parents than in some less desirable hall where there is no supervision.

The churches in America, in other words, are organized social centers, performing a vital function in the community and, what is most important, they were and still are, in many cases, the only social centers in this colonial country tending to develop a higher moral consciousness in America's young community life. The churches have turned the purely individualistic egotism of a colonial people, which had no roots anywhere, into a moral community spirit.

In America even the churches are not free from
the customary business attitude.   They advertise
their work extensively and compete with each other
all the time.   It is inevitable that many of their
activities are pure cant, pure convention; they reflect
a love of external respectability and they are not
altogether free from snobbishness.   The Episcopal
Church, like the English High Church, is considered
the most elegant and the most exclusive sect and
many people, including Jews who have made money,
attend this church because it may enhance their
social position.   In some ways churches in America
encourage an extremely narrow mental attitude, but
much that is worth while, much freedom of thought
and social justice, is alive in these institutions as
well.

American church life includes many varieties of
doctrine: from the Fundamentalists who take the
Bible literally, to very liberal sects with a clergy
(including some Lutheran ministers), who no longer
believe in any dogma, who preach the life of Christ
as the great Example, and the Quakers, who are
really churchless and believe in the doctrine of broth-
erly love.   All these faiths and beliefs of various
kinds and degrees find an outlet in church organizations, always independent of the state, which are very
much alive.   The outward forms which American
community life has assumed, as well as its value to
society, can be really appreciated only if one under-
stands the historical influence of these communities
on the colonials living in a colonial country.

M. J. Bonn expresses the situation very aptly
when he says that the taming of the frontiersmen
was the primary function of social forces in America.
The country has indeed created a neighborly indi-

vidual out of a pioneer, who lived on a farm; and migratory colonial workers, who every day lived somewhere else and performed some other job, developed into good citizens. Above all America has been faced with the problem of remolding these migratory individuals, who came together by accident, into members of a community, voluntarily acknowledging common laws and regulations. The churches are only one of the social forces which have contributed towards this end. Custom and convention are other powerful, though invisible factors molding this community life, and these invisible forces which, like the influence of the churches, originating in the East, have determined modes of life and have established unwritten laws of conduct among the people living on the prairies, in the new cities of the West. The smaller, the younger, and the more isolated these towns or settlements are, the greater is the power of convention. It seems almost as though people were afraid that their homes might disintegrate if they do not bow down to it. For economic developments are not the only causes which have contributed towards the general standardization in America, where the homes and the clothing and food, and the daily routine of life are standardized; the influence of convention has been equally important in this development.

At the same time convention controls the people's inner life; it determines a citizen's attitude towards his business and towards his family. Convention prescribes his duties as a good citizen, it molds his thoughts and his aims. Public opinion supervises him constantly, ever ready to make his private affairs public property. There is no privacy, no reserve in American provincial life, which is entirely controlled by convention, and any one offending against it, any one who defies public opinion, is no longer respectable.

American women are the strongest supporters of the church, of conventions and of social forces generally, in fact they are the third powerful influence regulating and controlling American life. They have retained the privileged position they occupied as a matter of course during the first decades of American development, when there were fewer women than men in the country and when the women's help was indispensable to the pioneers building their new homes in the wilderness. Women in America have retained this position, furthermore, because, as in all colonial countries, they are the natural protectors of morality, which would vanish if they did not keep the sacred fires burning.

American women owe their domestic supremacy to these colonial traditions—and all of them enjoy these privileges, whether they are the luxurious wives of men whose one aim in life seems to be to earn more money so that they shall have more to waste, or whether their husbands belong to the middle classes and they have plenty of work to do in their households. Even in such homes the husbands are willing to relieve their wives of the most arduous domestic tasks. Daughters, too, are given precedence over sons, and if parents cannot afford to send all their children to college the girls are given the money to go before the sons are considered. Women's position in America, as contrasted with Europe, is apparent even on the streets; when a family is getting onto a bus or a street car, or when they are crossing a crowded street corner, it is always the father, and not the mother, who carries the child.

And woe unto a man who dares approach a strange woman on the street, if she does not invite such familiarity; she may easily report him to the police and he may spend several days in jail as a result. American women enjoy more than equality, they occupy a position superior to the men. Married women whose children are old enough not to need constant care have more leisure than their husbands, who work extremely hard in their business or profession. Their leisure is increased by the fact that most men eat their luncheon away from home, and that women are spared a great deal of household care by clubs (and by the canning factories). Many social obligations which in Germany mean elaborate dinner parties in the home are much simpler in America, where people meet in men's or women's clubs for a short and informal lunch.

It is just as easy for women as for men to get a higher education and as I have mentioned, often girls rather than boys take advantage of this opportunity. For this reason women have the opportunity of playing a considerable rôle in public life; as a rule they are the chief promoters of music and literature; it is they who are actively engaged in social welfare work. The pacifist movement in America is very largely controlled by women. The women's influence through their numerous organizations in the churches, above all, is their chief source of moral and political power, which they now use not to tame the frontiersmen themselves as in colonial days, but to tame community life as a whole. Owing to the women's influence and their strict code of sexual ethics it has been possible, for instance, for prostitution to be abolished in a city like Chicago in the course of a few years, which is an astonishing achievement.

Prohibition, which has probably exercised a more far-reaching influence on morality than any other regulation affecting private life in America, is chiefly due to the women's efforts.

Germans returning home after a visit in America frequently take a mischievous delight in telling about the many drinks they enjoyed in the United States, where, despite prohibition, they had many opportunities to secure alcoholic beverages. Many Germans believe, therefore, that prohibition in America has failed completely. This is the prevailing attitude in Germany, where the progress of prohibition throughout the world is either discredited altogether or ironically scorned. Soon we Germans may have the doubtful glory of taking the lead among civilized European nations, as far as our freedom in unlimited alcohol traffic is concerned. Many German-Americans are as opposed to prohibition as the Germans, because they are now deprived of their beloved beer and, what is more important, they have lost the harmless sociability a glass of beer meant to them when they met. For older German-Americans, who cannot get accustomed to the colder Anglo-American forms of sociability, this has been a real loss, for near beer, which is now served in the German-American restaurant and clubs, is no real substitute.

Such negative opinions do not give a true picture of the real facts of the success of the movement. It is true, of course, that prohibition has not been entirely successful and this is only natural, for its administrators are not powerful enough to enforce it completely. Exceptional cases, in which the sale of alcohol is legal, have made it possible for many people to circumvent prohibition. Wine for medical purposes or for church sacraments, permitted despite prohibition, is doubtless more popular now than it was before the amendment went into effect. There are plenty of legitimate and illegitimate "old" stocks of alcoholic beverages on hand in the country. Homebrew (the Italians are particularly versed in the domestic manufacture of wine) is permitted within limits and the temptation to surpass them is great. America's frontiers above all are so extensive and her ports so numerous that a complete supervision is impossible.

An extensive smuggling trade has developed as a result of prohibition, the number of bootleggers actively engaged in business is considerable, and the demoralization which has followed is viewed with concern in America. Conditions, not unlike the smuggling which occurred during our period of compulsory state control of trade during and after the war, now prevail in America, where many people, otherwise conscientious respecters of the law, exploit this bootleg trade, successfully overcoming any pangs of conscience which they may have felt.

A large steamship company with vessels traveling between Germany and America is willing to discard the Stars and Stripes and fly the Panama flag, so that drinks can be served on board its ships. In some circles, especially among young people, it has become a regular sport to circumvent prohibition: in some college fraternities large quantities of whisky are consumed before celebrations of various kinds (for in public, during the dinners themselves, this is impossible). Even high school students of both

sexes in the dangerous large cities occasionally recognize no limits where this sport is concerned,
though among them, so far, such cases are exceptional.

The bootleggers themselves are a particularly demoralizing influence. Children, who have no idea
that they are doing wrong, are frequently employed
by them as outposts. When a bootlegger has the
bad luck to be shot by the police it is not unusual to
see a long procession of mourners following the
hearse: his death is considered an entirely honorable
professional accident and the risks involved in the
trade only tend to increase the price of the commodity sold, in fact these risks are taken into account when prices are fixed. The bootleggers are,
of course, a new element of corruption; they endanger the morale of the police, of administrative
bodies and of the politicians connected with these
bodies. People in America often jestingly remark
that prohibition cannot be abolished, because the
bootleggers now have as many political and financial
connections as the capitalists of the liquor trade once
had. It is now being seriously considered whether
the demoralizing effects of prohibition might be
diminished by some mitigation of the law which
need not, however, abolish prohibition as such. For
it is out of the question that prohibition will be
abolished in the immediate future, and there are
very good reasons why this is so.

One typically American reason why prohibition
will stay is the fact that it abolished saloons and sup-
pressed this source of political and moral corruption, which had been poisoning American life. Many
saloon owners were the agents and henchmen of
corrupt political bosses whose campaigns were

organized in the saloons themselves, which were also the recruiting quarters of all kinds of criminals. American life was tremendously purified when these institutions, which had been a real pest, were exterminated. The abolition of the saloons was a benefit to the country which none of the unfavorable effects of prohibition can counteract.

The saloons were fatal to labor. Innumerable workers wasted their hard-earned wages and ruined their families by just "stopping for a moment" on their way home to have "one glass" of liquor, which so often ended with a "round of drinks." The American worker has derived great material and moral benefits from the abolition of the saloons, and these benefits are, of course, not specifically American. We Germans are equally familiar with the sad picture of the worker who, with his pay envelope in his pocket, stops at the saloon for longer than he expected and whose anxious wife waits in vain for him and the money, without which she cannot buy bread for her children. It is the consensus of opinion in America that prohibition has greatly stimulated the progress of labor, not only because the worker has learned to save the money which he might otherwise have spent on drink, but because his general sobriety has increased his efficiency and enabled him to earn higher wages. Socially this has been the most important result brought about by prohibition and it is an achievement which other countries should consider as well.

Some distinguished American political economists very largely attribute the recent increase of production as well as the post-war prosperity in general to prohibition, and that their opinion is shared by a great many people is indicated by the fact that some

of the large employers' and workers' organizations
are now unitedly supporting prohibition because they
consider it a vital factor in the maintenance of the
country's wealth, and the workers' efficiency; they believe that prohibition has helped to increase the country's purchasing power and has contributed towards
the rise in wages and the increased productivity of
industry which has continued despite these high
wages. Business interests as a whole are no longer
opposed to prohibition. The saloons have been replaced by shops of various kinds. The breweries
have readjusted their output and are manufacturing
canned goods, ice or ice cream. Even the wine-
growers are satisfied, for their grapes are sold as
raisins or as ingredients for home-brews at high
prices, made possible because, under prohibition,
foreign wines cannot be imported into America.

Despite an extensive smuggling trade in alcoholic
beverages, and despite the bootleggers, prohibition
has quite evidently markedly decreased the consumption of alcohol in the United States. Even individuals who complain a great deal about this curtailment of their personal liberty are very economical
with their stocks of alcohol, which is, after all, very
hard to obtain, at least of good quality. The number of individuals revolting against prohibition is
smaller than it was at first and is still diminishing;
even in their homes these people now frequently serve
only one cocktail to each guest. In other private
social gatherings alcohol is no longer consumed at
all, and at public dinners it is, of course, excluded, so
that now most Americans drink very little. The
great masses of the people will become more and
more accustomed to doing without drink altogether
and there are many who are already accustomed to

abstinence. American life is being tamed by prohibition as well as by other things and the women and especially children are deriving the benefits of this development. The consideration of them, and of the coming generation which needs protection, is the strongest moral support of prohibition. This consideration of the children is more impressive and more important than all other economic or social factors which have supported the prohibition movement.

Social forces have tamed life in this colonial country; men's impulses have been restrained and severely controlled by moral laws. And even to-day, despite its material wealth and spaciousness, America is poor in the manner of colonial countries.

It is true, of course, that Americans have gained more than purely material benefits from their country's wealth and spaciousness; they have derived assurance and courage as well as cheerfulness and dignity. The degrading effects of poverty on individuals and on society as a whole, the demoralizing influence resulting from an atmosphere of fear and envy, of timidity and antagonism, were never more clear to me than in America, where the elevating moral effects of prosperity are so apparent. Americans seem to have acquired a democratic attitude of mind, due to this lack of degrading economic pressure, and this is perhaps even more important than their constitutional democracy. For this mental attitude makes crawling and bullying impossible. This attitude, which demands equality as far as human rights are concerned, influences American life as a whole. People respect each other, even children, who are regular little citizens in the miniature state consisting of the family as a whole, enjoy their recognized rights and responsibilities. It is the same in the schools, where the teachers do not maintain discipline and industry by punishing the pupils; they appeal to their sense of responsibility and to their ability to discipline themselves. In the universities the honor system takes the place of supervision. As I have said: people in America respect each other and they treat each other accordingly, they are courteous and considerate, cheerful and kindly, and a visitor is made to feel this friendly atmosphere again and again in small ways. "Keep smiling," a rule which is proclaimed everywhere, is actually followed in America and is not merely a mask. It is often said that Americans as a whole are more superficial than other people and for this reason they can more easily overcome the disagreeable sides of life. It may be true that they have not acquired as much book learning as other peoples, but out of their general feeling of security they have in any case developed the great art of not taking their troubles too seriously. Americans do not let themselves become depressed, they are not easily "downed" by their worries. Grown-up Americans like and know how to be cheerful and joyous, like children.

But the life of the average American is only superficially full of interests. Technical progress has made this possible, but underneath his life is empty. What does he gets out of life? He has the movies instead of the theater, he has a radio and a victrola instead of real music. He reads a magazine instead of a book—and no one could call these American magazines intellectual products; they are compiled with great efficiency—shallowness and dullness are apparently necessary for a large circulation—and there are some with a million subscribers. What else fills up the American's life? He dances; both men and women are passionately attached to passionless dancing. Perhaps Americans dance everywhere and anywhere at all times of the day because they are not familiar with the joy of quiet chats in cafés as we know it in Europe. Their dances are daring in form but not full of excitement; they dance seriously and sometimes they chew gum in time with the music. How else do the Americans occupy their time? They are fond of sports, which are, in fact, the American's great passion and they not only enjoy the games they play themselves, which refresh and strengthen their bodies, but they are far more interested in the sporting events for which they pay and which they attend as inactive spectators. When the hired teams of Jamestown and Jones City meet, the audience trembles, for every one feels that the honor of his city is at stake. And when a great professional baseball player, who earns huge sums of money, defends his championship he is the national hero. The front page of the newspapers is full of it when Babe Ruth has a slight fever, and it is considered elevating even to read of his prowess in the game.

But even great baseball events do not happen every day and as, so far, not enough inventions have been made in the line of entertainments, the average American—I am not speaking of exceptional types—must fill his life chiefly with business interests. Business is his passion and he does not retire until old age actually forces him to do so. Retirement means giving up business associations and often a man's position. And what is there for a retired business man to do in the residential section of his city which, after all, is a village occupied only by women and children from nine in the morning until five o'clock in the afternoon? American men want to live down town in a business atmosphere where everything is constantly moving.

This sense of hurry has permeated American homes; the women and even the children are imbued with it. Americans do not know what leisure is; they want to be on the go all the time; they want something to be happening every minute. This constant rush is not hard work for them; everything not directly concerned with their business or profession is considered play. "Playing round the house," they call it, when they clean their car or fix the shutters or their electric lighting system in the evening or on Sundays. The main point is that no moment is wasted and a great many Americans, including high school and college boys, consider any conversation which does not concern some specific aim or problem as a great waste of time. These boys do not know what to do with themselves when they are not playing some game or trying out a new wave-length on their radio. As a result of this restless attitude many mature Americans have developed some hobby, some secondary occupation, which amuses them, whether it be photography or automobile racing or some other activity, for active they must be. Earning money, too, can be a hobby.

Wealthy people in America give large sums of money to foundations of various kinds; it does not seem at all contradictory to them to amass their wealth in a ruthless manner only to give it away later. In fact public opinion demands this generosity which is supposed to show that these rich people are good citizens. Besides, even under the most luxurious standards of living there is a limit to what a man can spend and it seems unnecessary to save all his money for his children. Too much inherited wealth is not considered advisable; it often weakens the children's energy, and besides they do not really need it for they can make money for themselves. This is the attitude of even moderately wealthy Americans, but the realization that they do not actually have to earn so much makes them none the less active. In America activity is the highest law of life and even ministers and other intellectual workers hardly ever pause to collect their thoughts. From a lecture they hurry to a meeting, and thence to a session of the boys' club—that is business.

By hurrying and rushing Americans try to cover up the monotony of life, but because they vaguely sense that their existence is colorless they make tremendous efforts to substitute something for this lack of brightness. Nowhere in the world are masonic organizations as important, and nowhere is their function as superficial as it is in America. There are other secret lodges and societies as well, modeled after the masonic ones. They are all secret societies with no real secret, which serve only the one purpose of camouflaging a colorful life. The members proudly wear emblems in their buttonholes, and the annual meetings of these societies, which are really nothing but pleasure tours for most of the men attending, are a great sight. Twenty, thirty or even forty thousand members congregate, dressed in gorgeous uniforms with swords and plumed hats, or in fantastic costumes with peaked shoes and very wide, gayly colored, breeches, and red fezzes. They travel around the country for two weeks dressed as Turks or as historical soldiers, and when the masquerade is over they go back home as tamed and respectable citizens and resume their ceaseless efforts to sell real estate.

But despite these efforts the average American has a vague feeling that something is lacking in his life, and he gropes for it without knowing exactly what it is. With the exception of individuals who are happy in some faith or whose home life is unusually satisfying and harmonious, Americans harbor a feeling of dissatisfaction which prevents them from being fundamentally at peace and they are restless, like the wanderers they were when they first came to their colonial country. This lack of repose is the real reason why they change their residence and their profession so frequently. But they cannot overcome their dissatisfaction, because, even if they move geographically, they are only changing their outward environment, their outward activity, and their inner life remains just as unsettled as it was.

DEVELOPMENTS OF THE FUTURE

AMERICANS who sense the emptiness of their colonial existence, who realize the poverty of their mental inheritance and who appreciate that they lack the joys and the doubts of an older culture, are not usually discouraged. In fact with their usual optimism they justify themselves by saying that after all they are a young people. But this is not true. For why should Englishmen or Germans, or Italians who have come together here be less mature than their fellow countrymen in old Europe? America is a young country it is true, but when they say, as they frequently do, that there has been so much which had to be done in this new country that no time was left to cultivate beauty—their statement is erroneous. Why do they need automobiles before they buy pianos? Why are radios more important for them than books and pictures?

Why—and this question is probably fundamental for all colonial countries—why, I ask, are Americans so productive in material, technical or administrative achievements, and why, until recently, have they produced so little as far as beauty and mental progress is concerned? Hundreds of thousands, or even millions, of the European immigrants in America came from the most musical countries of our continent, but their musical inheritance has found no creative expression in the United States. Negro music developed. But what about these musical Europeans in the United States? Older people never lose their love of music and their longing follows them to the grave. The younger generation has very largely, however, lost this inheritance and as far as their understanding for music is concerned they all seem to be of English descent. And music is only one example for other arts and intellectual pursuits have suffered a similar fate.

The country is too prosperous and this is reflected in its cultural developments as well as along other lines. Material prosperity covers up an inner void. Probably the American atmosphere is a handicap to cultural progress,—this atmosphere in which the acquisition of wealth and the realization of material aims are the great criteria of success. The business man is the representative type of American, he is the incarnation of the national spirit, and any one harboring ambitions other than business success is considered a poor devil and a fool—first he is considered "queer" by his fellows and finally he himself comes to think that something is wrong with him. This attitude is beginning to permeate Germany as well; where we pityingly call a man of this kind theoretical the Americans call him a high-brow.

Even children are brought up in this atmosphere. And then there is a double lack in America: cultural contributions are neither given with devotion nor received with interest. The general public feels no cultural obligation for "culturally productive receptivity," as Alfred Weber so aptly called this attitude of mind causing the public willingly to participate in intellectual or artistic creation. Even if a greater part of the American public had more understanding for these things, there would be no time, no leisure, in the restlessness and rush of life, for people to concentrate on them. Creative spirits, therefore, are put off the track right at the beginning of their careers; they take up professions where success and recognition are assured. It is difficult for any germs of culture to mature in this atmosphere.

Scholars seeking the truth in an attic or artists who are willing to suffer deprivations while they try to give shape to their idea, are not exactly the vogue in Germany either, where complete devotion to some unpragmatic creative idea is no longer the fashion. In America, as can be readily imagined, attic rooms, and a lack of coal and food are particularly unpopular. In fact public opinion heartily disapproves of them and this disapproval of such deprivation is widespread. A young writer whom I met had traveled in the Orient and had written about his experiences, but no publisher would buy his book for none were interested. But when he became a staff reporter for a large news agency he was suddenly greatly respected by his relatives and friends, for now he was in the newspaper business. Whether he manufactured pins or news made very little difference, the main point was that he was doing a regular job, as he was expected to do. This attitude is very general. College professors who want to earn more money and become successful department store owners or high school teachers who give up teaching for the same reason are not unusual, but it cannot be said that such cases promise much for the study of classical philology.

Nevertheless it is clear that America is now in a transition stage. Her purely colonial period is over and as her people become crystallized as a nation they are beginning to reach out for new aims towards which they are striving. Many people believe that a great change has occurred during the last ten or fifteen years and that this change is still going on.

A new development, a new will, is beginning to permeate America's consciousness. The first settlement and the distribution of free land, which was of the greatest economic and social importance, may possibly result in a great, perhaps unconscious, change, of the country's mental development as well. "Formerly," an educated business man said to me, "our restlessness found an outlet in the loneliness of the prairies. Now that they have been given away, our unsettled state of mind, like some strange and compelling impulse, may cause us to find our way into another loneliness, into the great loneliness of thought and art."

America is in a transition stage. The times are passed when a colonial could find an outlet for his energy in rooting out trees, in making the land arable, in building railroads or factories. After these primary tasks had been performed Americans concentrated on the acquisition of knowledge, on the dissemination of information and on practical education of various kinds. These three things became a watchword, advertised with every possible art and every possible effort. Practical training is now being pursued by large sections of the population, and Americans, both young and old, are devoting themselves to this training with the disciplined energy with which they pursue other forms of business. These studies are not in the least imbued with the passionate speculative ardor with which many young Germans bury themselves in their books in the hope of finding out what makes the world go round. Practical knowledge is what these young Americans want (as I have previously mentioned), for they feel that they must be able to meet growing competition. This attitude is the starting point, but it will not be the ultimate result of this thirst for knowledge; even to-day it is not the exclusive aim. The material wealth and the increasing prosperity of the last few years will ultimately bear fruit as far as the attitude towards knowledge is concerned.

The thirst for information in America is satisfied by all kinds of scientific data and material, in pamphlet or book form, which are distributed free of charge or at a low cost by public services or by organizations interested. Moreover, American libraries have been expanded enormously; the more important cities and the larger universities have remarkably complete collections of books from all over the world; there are huge library buildings in which every possible facility and comfort for the reader has been installed. These libraries have large funds at their disposal so that they can go on expanding, all of which makes a German feel even more concerned about the unavoidable deterioration of German libraries during and since the war. The magnificent City Library in New York is comparable only with the British Museum, but whereas the latter is used only for quiet and intensive research work the former is devoted to the whole population of this city of eight million people. Books are loaned out with the minimum possible red tape and the large reading rooms, like oases in the midst of the bustling activity of the city, are invitingly open to the public from early in the morning until ten at night. The New York Library is the model for similar institutions in various parts of the country; every medium-sized town and every prairie village now has at least a modest library of its own. The Carnegie Foundation has done a great work by contributing as large a sum to every city wanting a library as the citizens of the town were willing to raise themselves. This system, started by the Carnegie Foundation, caused a regular race for libraries. Now donations from the Foundation are no longer necessary for even without them no city wants to be without a Public Library, which seems as indispensable to-day as running water and electric light.

All these educational institutions indicate that the country's wealth, which, at first, was the greatest obstacle to its mental progress, is beginning, after all, to stimulate an intellectual development.

There are not, it is true, many museums in America, but the Metropolitan Museum in New York has a magnificent collection, including not only very fine pictures by European artists, purchased in Europe by private individuals and given to the Museum, but a collection of Chinese art unequaled in size or beauty in any museum in the world. America is in a position to acquire anything that money will buy, but there must be some leaders who know how to discriminate.

Farther west, in Chicago, for instance, where there is a remarkable natural history museum, only a very modest Art Institute has been established. One is quite startled, in this Institute, suddenly to encounter beautiful gothic façades and portals, all true imitations of European originals, which seem to emphasize, somehow, what Americans lack. But a European oversensitiveness of this kind has nothing to do with the situation. Whereas all over Europe there are visibile artistic traces of historical traditions, which are (or were) part and parcel of Europe's system of values, in America these are traces of incipient beginnings. And the fact that thousands of Americans go to Europe every year means a constant encouragement of those tendencies. Therefore, it is more important to appreciate these new attempts of a fuller intellectual life than to register what America still lacks along these lines. Many medium-sized towns are now making a touching effort to organize museums; they have also adopted new methods of teaching the public how to appreciate art. In Dayton, Ohio, pictures are loaned, like books from the libraries; people may take them home and hang them up, free of charge, for a certain period. At first there was some feeling against this system, which, so it was thought, might damage the pictures, but these objections were overcome on the grounds that any one caring for pictures enough to borrow them would be careful. This system of loaning pictures has been successful beyond all expectation; many people become so used to having them in their homes that they want to own them or other works of art. The museum, therefore, installed a sales department for the benefit of the artist and the purchaser, and now painters are particularly glad to send their pictures to this medium-sized city. This work is just beginning but it is very promising.

As far as music is concerned the situation is similar. In the large cities, there is, of course, always a sufficiently interested public to maintain really good performances, and attract the best great European artists. But what is more significant is the fact that, according to leading European musicians, the instruments used by the Philadelphia Orchestra, for instance, probably surpass even the instruments used by the Vienna orchestra (a result of the country's wealth!). Current efforts everywhere to encourage a love and an understanding of music among the population as a whole by first class public perform-

ances are very significant. All these efforts are only
beginnings, which do not contradict but only supple-
ment what I have said, but as such they are extremely
important. They should not, however, be overestimated; for so far America is still dominated by an
ambition for material outward success. But as a
whole this success has already been so great that the
people are gradually beginning to reach out for new
aims. America's great architectural achievements,
which are so expressive of a real creative art, are the
outstanding example of what these new aims may
be like.

Can wealth, imperiously defying the world, acquire culture simply by paying the price? Certainly
not. On the contrary, wealth may be a real obstacle
towards this end; but obviously wealth can, if it
chooses, encourage artistic and intellectual creation,
for an unheated attic room is not absolutely necessary. In fact this uncomfortable environment may
be such a disadvantage for an artist or a scholar
that he cannot produce anything. America is slowly
and tentatively beginning to prove, on the other
hand, to what an extent wealth and comfort can
stimulate scientific progress. Pure research, without
practical aims, is rare in America. Instructors at the
universities and colleges do not, as a rule, try to discover truth for truth's sake; most of them try instead to disseminate as much practical knowledge as
possible among their students. Professors living in
this pragmatic American atmosphere have not succeeded in becoming intellectual, political or moral
leaders of their community. Their relatively small
salaries indicate their modest position in the eye of
public opinion in this country, where the number of
dollars earned is the criterion of success or failure.

The average salary for a young university instructor amounts to $3,000 (which is about equal to the annual wages of a skilled worker). More experienced professors, on the average, earn between $4,000 and $5,000. Higher salaries do not seem necessary, for scholars would find it very hard to escape into another profession. But a plan, just started at Chicago, seems to me to be significant for the future. The University of Chicago wanted to build up a first-class medical school and an effort was made to attract distinguished physicians, who would be willing to give up their private practices and concentrate all their time on teaching. The University announced its willingness to pay a salary of $10,000 to the directors of this new medical department, but there were no applicants at all for these positions, as really good private practices are, of course, much more remunerative. The university by no means gave up the plan, but went on collecting funds for this new department and for other scientific work. Very soon more than a hundred million dollars had accumulated. Then a new announcement was made offering salaries of $25,000 for this medical work. It is probable that this sum will attract the type of physician wanted, but if it does not the university will offer more, that is all. This is, of course, a specific case, but it is not an isolated one.

The University of Chicago, furthermore, in the Yerkes Observatory, owns the largest telescope in the world; a few decades ago the place where it now stands was a part of the Indians' hunting ground. The considerable number of other scientific institutes in the United States indicates, in the first place, what huge sums of money are available for scientific purposes and that, in the second place, America is beginning increasingly to spend money for work of this kind. So far applied science has been given the most extensive financial support, for practical science appeals most strongly to the Americans' pragmatic attitude and besides practical research can be more actively encouraged by money than other branches of science. America will probably compete with Europe, first of all, in the field of applied science, for laboratories and other equipment, without which this work is impossible, are available in practically unlimited quantities in the United States. A really scientific spirit is developing in America along these lines, a spirit which is not nurtured by scholars in unheated attic rooms either, but by well-paid scientists, whose high salaries relieve them of petty worries, and whose social position is nearly as good as any stockbroker's. There is a similar development in the field of economics; some of the large banks employ highly trained theoretical economists, whose opinion of the theories current in Germany during the inflation period, and of their practical application, is anything but flattering. Pure science, philosophy particularly, will probably be the last research subject to be extensively developed in the United States.

But the fact that an intellectual unrest and curiosity is gradually being awakened and is becoming a factor in American life is far more important for life itself than all these tangible beginnings. The monkey case in Tennessee was discussed with ironical surprise in Europe, where people could hardly credit the report that American states can pass laws prohibiting the teaching of the theory of evolution in primary and high schools. These laws are, in fact, really a reaction to the intellectual unrest which is beginning to stir. In communities where this unrest is considered a danger by the solid majority, an effort is made to root it out with the same uncompromising severity which defeated the anarchistic egotism of the frontiersmen, which persecutes communistic and syndicalistic ideas. The same severity is applied to this mental unrest which brought about prohibition, but which has never yet been expressed in an effort to abolish the contemptible exploitation of child labor.

Such a solid majority does not admit that it must respect intellectual freedom, with the result that the theory of evolution is banned as a public danger at a time, when in Europe, it has long since ceased to be a basic problem or even a debatable question. But as far as America's future is concerned, so it seemed to me, the indignation felt by educated people all over America about this case was far more significant than the case itself. American intellectuals felt themselves disgraced, not because of the theory itself, but because of the attack on intellectual liberty which the case involved and the dictatorial manner in which a political body could decide such intellectual questions. In all parts of the country, therefore, from the East to the West, educated people were agitated about this case and the passion with which they defended intellectual liberty indicates that there are small groups of people everywhere in America who, despite convention and the unintellectual atmosphere, possess and value mental liberty.

Any description of the United States would be incomplete which did not mention the fact that there are everywhere, even in medium-sized or small cities, people whose mental habits and intellectual interests are like those of an educated European—these people are really like Europeans, fundamentally, except that they happen to live in an American environment with its many opportunities. Intellectual unrest has sprung up among people of this kind, and is expressed in many ways.

In America there is no youth movement like the one we know in Germany. Young people, who possibly approach the German type, are quite surprised when they hear about the German movement: they cannot understand why German youth takes itself so very seriously and why it talks about itself so much. American young people lack the impulses prompting such a movement. It would never occur to them to resist suppression in the schools and in the home, because no such suppression exists in America where youth is free (some say it is too free) and where young people live their own lives, which are respected by the older generation. As a whole the breach between succeeding generations, the conflicts between fathers and sons, do not occur in the United States.

Nevertheless, new impulses are stirring among a part of the youth of America; not in opposition but spontaneously, a new desire to delve more deeply into problems as individuals has been awakened. This tendency is chiefly expressed by a number of male and female college students and has been particularly stimulated by a group of liberal theologians in some of the colleges and universities. Despite the fact that most of the students at these institutions are entirely unproblematical natures (the country is too prosperous!), groups of students in all of them are realizing that, despite its great prosperity, the country is faced with many unsolved problems. These young men and young women are conscious of their own moral responsibility towards these problems. Social questions, race problems and pacifism become immediate and urgent personal considerations in their own lives. There have always been a number of individual men or women who have been personally conscious of these problems, but the new phase in this development of thought is the fact that now these young people are collectively interested in these questions—they feel a group solidarity in their desire some day, when they have become mature men and women, to apply their more profound insight to these problems. These students, therefore, represent an element which is full of hope for the intellectual unrest of the future. Similar tendencies are beginning to be felt among groups of idealistic women as well.

The most significant symptom that a new force is really awakening in American life, where as a rule convention still rules supreme, is the beginning of a "Bohème," of a group of "unconventionals," who always lead a community when an active protest against convention, against the spirit in power and against traditional habits of life, is beginning to develop. Books, such as those by Sinclair Lewis, are symptomatic of this development, for at times almost photographically he overemphasizes the narrowness and smallness of American life, thus causing many people to become conscious, for the first time, of certain inevitable problems confronting their country. The work of other writers is full of uncompromising irony and satire. Groups of literary people and courageous magazines mean a vital intellectual, political and social opposition to the powers that be.

And even if the number of Americans influenced by these views is still relatively small, even if the Babbitts are in the majority, there is no doubt but that these small groups of people are keeping the fires of this sacred unrest alive; they stand out against America of to-day and represent, in fact, the beginning of America of to-morrow.

WHAT OF EUROPE?

And what of Europe? This question, arising again and again in the mind of a European, continues to depress and to mortify him. America is progressing, whereas Europe, during the last decade, has retrogressed step by step.

The purely economic development of the old world and the new have not been decisive alone in this progress and this decline. America's wealth simply increased while Europe became poorer. This was Europe's fault as well as her Fate. America developed methods of increasing her wealth, whereas Europe fell behind in many ways; the old world forgot to adjust itself to the world changes, it forgot to follow, to keep step with her, to go beyond these changes. To a certain extent this was due to Europe's unhealthy condition, which is also causing great distress, but which need not be permanent, which will not last forever. The war and the post-war period were poor teachers of economics for European countries, and the most primitive economic facts were forgotten in various European countries during these difficult years. People forgot that it is uneconomical to spend more than one earns; that healthy economic conditions must be based on healthy financial conditions, and that a country's finances can not remain healthy unless the necessary taxes are paid. It was temporarily forgotten, also, that the products of industry cannot find a market if the customers' purchasing power is undermined and that, for the same reason, appreciable wage reductions, even if they are possible, do not pay in the end, because they ruin the domestic market. People in Europe also forgot that currency inflation and import restrictions are only a temporary makeshift, and a poor one at that. People in Europe forgot that a country's ability to produce must be proved in a fair race and that in the end the greater ability must win. Necessity will, however, in time, force Europe to remember all these things it had forgotten. In fact, European countries are already beginning to recall them.

There is another more decisive fact. Americans have become increasingly conscious to what extent their economic progress is based upon the fact that their vast country constitutes one great market, while Europe, on the contrary, has been increasingly split up into small national markets.

The Peace Treaties created new frontiers, thousands of kilometers in length; all of Eastern and a part of Central Europe are like the Balkans. European countries have committed the folly of cutting themselves off from each other. After the first year of the war, Friedrich Naumann expressed the belief that the trenches would last forever, for, he said, new frontier entrenchments would continue after the war to separate all those countries which might, possibly, wage future wars against each other. That prediction was a dreadful mistake on the part of this otherwise clear-minded man. Yet, what the postwar period has done to Europe (quite aside from the Peace Treaties) proves that this apocalyptic vision was not so far from true. To-day Europe is burdened by travel and passport restrictions, by restrictions limiting the activities of traveling business men and the establishment of branch offices by commercial and industrial concerns in foreign countries, as well as by import and export prohibitions. The disastrous effects of these restrictions are intensified by the currency depreciation in various countries which entirely destroyed, for all practical purposes, the uniformity of the pre-war world currency. The effects of these restrictions are aggravated also by the race into which European countries have apparently entered to eclipse each other in the increase of their import duties. Such is Europe to-day.

It is strangely contradictory that as Europe grew less powerful, because of the breaking up into many small nations, these nations themselves seemed increasingly to crave isolated nationalistic power, whereas they had formerly constituted one economic unit. The Austrian Succession States are the crassest example of this tendency. Now that they have been torn apart into separate economic units they apparently want above all—with the artificial aid of protectionism—to include, in their limited economic area, all the activities which they lost to one of their neighbors. Countries retaining a spinning industry after the separation of the Austro-Hungarian Empire seem to feel that they must have a weaving industry as well, and countries which saved their weaving centers apparently believe that their national honor depends upon the establishment of a spinning trade. And the countries which, after the separation, retained the smallest industrial equipment seemed to feel a great urge to build up an industry with the help of all the arts of high tariffs. Hungary would be positively embarrassed if Hungarian ladies were forced indefinitely to do without national Hungarian safety pins. As a matter of fact, all of Europe is acting on the principle of these national Hungarian safety pins. Europe is permeated by a sense of economic nationalism, an ambitious desire for power, which finds satisfaction in inefficient methods of production. The people themselves carry the burden. They pay the high import duties supporting artificial industrial creations, they pay the superprices as a compensation for the increased European production costs. The fateful watchword in Europe is now *autarchy,* which is gradually acquiring an ironical flavor, for this desire to provide for itself results in a system of not being provided for at all: prices are rising, the quality of goods is deteriorating, the competitive ability is weakening, and unemployment is increasing. But even this need not and will not last indefinitely, for after all Europe is gradually growing together again. Though, at first, the war apparently destroyed what was left of European unity, it has now united European countries by a common fate; all of them feel the same burden of debt. For Germany's reparation payments are no longer an isolated consideration. Interest payments and refunding of war debts, which the victorious allies owe each other (practically speaking, which they owe the United States), interests and refunding of the capital which they are now all trying to borrow from the United States—all these indebtednesses are, in fact, economically the same. They are causing all European countries to make the same claims. All must demand the same freedom to sell their products, the only way in which, ultimately, the majority of these payments can be made.

This need of foreign markets is gradually forcing Europe to set the world an example by beginning to remove the tariff walls which are restraining trade. Government politicians in European countries are still behind the times. Therefore, these necessary economic reforms will not be realized as soon as they should be. It is a comforting thought that in the interim the peoples concerned again have time to think of Europe as a unit. Economic experiences are encouraging this change of attitude, for the European victors in the Great War have learned the meaning of Pyrrhus' exclamation when he said that, "Another Victory of this kind and we shall be lost."

Gradually people are beginning to realize also that the impoverishment of any one country means a similar fate for its neighbors, and that a country can progress more quickly if its neighbor, too, is progressing. Materialistic economic considerations of this kind cannot really unite Europe any more than loud economic conferences or all kinds of organizations or associations of the various countries concerned, can do so. United Europe is a question of conviction, a question of developing a will, which may be transmuted into action and result in such a unity. A country's politics are its destiny, for no matter how much tragedy is concealed behind a few dry foreign-trade statistics or behind unemployment figures—the deeper pathos of this tragedy is not really felt unless there is good will among men. And this good will must be learned afresh, must be felt anew.

Europe's mental condition is now far more depressing than her economic deficiencies and her geographical disruption. I should like to repeat what I said before: it is completely erroneous to imagine that America of to-day is what Europe will be like to-morrow. 450 million people live in Europe and they obviously lack the breadth and spaciousness which Americans enjoy. It is our destiny to live in meagerness and narrowness. It may be possible that in future the prime necessities may be more fairly distributed among the peoples of Europe—but Europe will never have the great freedom of open spaces. Present conditions in America, therefore, do not indicate what Europe will be like in the future, but if one has seen America one seems to see Europe of to-day more clearly, as though through a magnifying glass. If one deducts from America her happy colonial plenty and considers only her colonial emptiness, then what is left looks like Europe—like Europe lighted up everywhere. The difference is, however, that America does not yet possess, but is gradually acquiring, what we once owned and have seen abandoned. Europe, the mother continent, on the contrary, is being increasingly permeated by the spirit of her colony, although, because of her smaller supply of material goods, this spirit will never bring forth the same results.

The best forces in America are trying to overcome the present state of shallowness; many of the finest types of Americans, who have retained their old moral European inheritance, have not, in fact, ever been affected by this shallowness. Pre-war Europe, on the other hand, was submerged by it, and in 1914 the catastrophe broke loose, because no moral forces were alive in Europe which could stop it. Nostra culpa, nostra maxima culpa, and who in Europe has the courage to absolve himself? And who would dare to say, all hopeful signs notwithstanding, that Europe is really on the road to overcoming this inertia which is the outgrowth of her spiritual shallowness? I think we should seriously consider the lessons we can learn from America, for, regarding the various facts of poverty in her private and public life, I think we shall realize how poor

Europe has become. Europe has not declined during her period of misfortune only, no matter how disastrous the last ten years may have been, but during the whole period of material wealth before the war. As far as some human values are concerned Europe is really poorer than America, because in Europe materialism is more materialistic, brutality is more brutal, and the dullness of life is even duller than in America, where spaciousness and plenty seem to soften and mellow these traits. But it cannot be claimed as an excuse and as a compensation for Europe that "the country is too prosperous."

For Europe is indeed not well off; on the contrary, problems which America is too prosperous to feel, which the country's prosperity has prevented from becoming vital and absorbing issues, are not intellectual pastimes in Europe but basic problems on which Europe's very existence depends. These problems, which include such issues as the state and the belief in the state, the social order and human dignity, are the quintessence of the present European crisis and Europe's future depends upon whether enough ethical passion to solve these problems will be awakened or not.

Europe must solve them herself; she cannot expect a solution to come from America, for America is not yet ready to help. Europe must shape its destiny in its own way, and it is good that this should be so, for it indicates that Europe is faced with tasks other than merely serving Americans as a destination for their summer outing, or as a museum, or a cabinet full of curios.

It is necessary to look at a map to appreciate Europe's size, for then one realizes how small Europe, covering only a thirteenth part of the globe, really is. Europe is really—only one of Asia's peninsulas and on this modest peninsula off the Asiatic coast more than a quarter of the world's population is crowded together. Europe has sent her population to all corners of the globe and what is even more important is the fact that for two or three hundred years Europe impressed her hallmark on the greater part of the inhabited world. Europe's culture and customs, its categories of thought and its economic systems and modes of life controlled a huge, growing part of the ecumenical world. For a period of two or three centuries Europe was the world's criterion of values. Herein lies the greatness of this Asiatic peninsula which we call Europe and which is comparable only to Athens' influence on the Mediterranean world in antiquity. And Europe's responsibilities as well as her tasks have not yet been exhausted.

One thing, at least, should be remembered: it matters very little how high office buildings rise into the sky. The decisive thing is always how profoundly individuals are rooted in spiritual things. The strength of the heart is the decisive factor.

To a German returning from America Germany seems like an idyl. The customs officers are the first reminder of home; they come on board at Southampton and spend many hours, or a half day, fulfilling a beautiful, entirely useless ceremony consisting of pasting green labels on the passengers' baggage. There is no thought of any real payment of duty or any serious examination of the luggage, but they live up to the outward forms to their hearts' content. The customs officials are inefficient, the Americans say, as one stands around patiently at first, and then impatiently. I am afraid that they will discover this lack of efficiency in other phases of this idyl later on.

Then the automobile in Hamburg nearly runs over a man: chauffeurs and pedestrians are still dilettantes in Germany. Later, in the station, it requires a moment's thought to recall that these small railroad carriages are not toys, but are used to transport real people and real freight and that they are like all the trains in Germany. Everything, not only the trains at home, seems somewhat small and somewhat narrow: like an idyl indeed. But then, in the train, one sees North German women again for the first time after the journey. They are blond, somewhat austere and simple and are not wearing the prescribed silk dress, in fact they are not standardized at all, they are individuals with an individual character, like home in general. And as one travels through Germany one forgets the entanglements and confusions of the present and comes closer to the root of things. Mayence, Cologne, with its "Thousand Year Exhibit," which is not a part of the small narrow idyl. This exhibit is the expression of great, lasting and immeasurable wealth; beautiful objects have been brought from old "burgers" houses, from churches, from city halls, from a thousand secluded places. They are treasures from Germany's depths. Is it possible that such beauty belongs only to the past and not to the future? Is it possible that Germany represents only an idyl and no strength? No, this better Germany is vital. It will continue in so far as we harbor the same will and the same sincerity to mold the adversities and the hardness of the day into beauty as our forefathers did in the past.

THE END

Foreign Travelers in America
1810–1935

AN ARNO PRESS COLLECTION

Archer, William. **America To-Day**: Observations and Reflections. 1899.

Belloc, Hilaire. **The Contrast**. 1924.

[Boardman, James]. **America, and the Americans**. By a Citizen of the World. 1833.

Bose, Sudhindra. **Fifteen Years in America**. 1920.

Bretherton, C. H. **Midas, Or, The United States and the Future**. 1926.

Bridge, James Howard (Harold Brydges). **Uncle Sam at Home**. 1888.

Brown, Elijah (Alan Raleigh). **The Real America**. 1913.

Combe, George. **Notes on the United States Of North America During a Phrenological Visit in 1838-9-40**. 1841. 2 volumes in one.

D'Estournelles de Constant, Paul H. B. **America and Her Problems**. 1915.

Duhamel, Georges. **America the Menace**: Scenes from the Life of the Future. Translated by Charles Miner Thompson. 1931.

Feiler, Arthur. **America Seen Through German Eyes**. Translated by Margaret Leland Goldsmith. 1928.

Fidler, Isaac. **Observations on Professions, Literature, Manners, and Emigration, in the United States and Canada, Made During a Residence There in 1832**. 1833.

Fitzgerald, William G. (Ignatius Phayre). **Can America Last?** A Survey of the Emigrant Empire from the Wilderness to World-Power Together With Its Claim to "Sovereignty" in the Western Hemisphere from Pole to Pole. 1933.

Gibbs, Philip. **People of Destiny**: Americans As I Saw Them at Home and Abroad. 1920.

Graham, Stephen. **With Poor Immigrants to America**. 1914.

Griffin, Lepel Henry. **The Great Republic**. 1884.

Hall, Basil. **Travels in North America in the Years 1827 and 1828**. 1829. 3 volumes in one.

Hannay, James Owen (George A. Birmingham). **From Dublin to Chicago**: Some Notes on a Tour in America. 1914.

Hardy, Mary (McDowell) Duffus. **Through Cities and Prairie Lands:** Sketches of an American Tour. 1881.

Holmes, Isaac. **An Account of the United States of America,** Derived from Actual Observation, During a Residence of Four Years in That République, Including Original Communications. [1823].

Ilf, Ilya and Eugene Petrov. **Little Golden America:** Two Famous Soviet Humorists Survey These United States. Translated by Charles Malamuth. 1937.

Kerr, Lennox. **Back Door Guest.** 1930.

Kipling, Rudyard. **American Notes.** 1899.

Leng, John. **America in 1876:** Pencillings During a Tour in the Centennial Year, With a Chapter on the Aspects of American Life. 1877.

Longworth, Maria Theresa (Yelverton). **Teresina in America.** 1875. 2 volumes in one.

Low, A[lfred] Maurice. **America at Home.** [1908].

Marshall, W[alter] G[ore]. **Through America:** Or, Nine Months in the United States. 1881.

Mitchell, Ronald Elwy. **America:** A Practical Handbook. 1935.

Moehring, Eugene P. **Urban America and the Foreign Traveler, 1815-1855.** With Selected Documents on 19th-Century American Cities. 1974.

Muir, Ramsay. **America the Golden:** An Englishman's Notes and Comparisons. 1927.

Price, M[organ] Philips. **America After Sixty Years:** The Travel Diaries of Two Generations of Englishmen. 1936.

Sala, George Augustus. **America Revisited:** From the Bay of New York to the Gulf of Mexico and from Lake Michigan to the Pacific. 1883. 3rd edition. 2 volumes in one.

Saunders, William. **Through the Light Continent;** Or, the United States in 1877-8. 1879. 2nd edition.

Smith, Frederick [Edwin] (Lord Birkenhead). **My American Visit.** 1918.

Stuart, James. **Three Years in North America.** 1833. 2 volumes in one.

Teeling, William. **American Stew.** 1933.

Vivian, H. Hussey. **Notes of a Tour in America from August 7th to November 17th, 1877.** 1878.

Wagner, Charles. **My Impressions of America.** Translated by Mary Louise Hendee. 1906.

Wells, H. G. **The Future in America:** A Search After Realities. 1906.